TRIALS
and
TRIBULATIONS
of a
TRAVELLING PROSTITUTE

ANDREW MACKAY

authorHOUSE

AuthorHouse™ UK
1663 Liberty Drive
Bloomington, IN 47403 USA
www.authorhouse.co.uk
Phone: 0800.197.4150

© 2018 Andrew Mackay. All rights reserved.

No part of this book may be reproduced, stored in a retrieval system, or transmitted by any means without the written permission of the author.

Published by AuthorHouse 07/26/2018

ISBN: 978-1-5462-9441-2 (sc)
ISBN: 978-1-5462-9442-9 (e)

Print information available on the last page.

Any people depicted in stock imagery provided by Getty Images are models, and such images are being used for illustrative purposes only.
Certain stock imagery © Getty Images.

This book is printed on acid-free paper.

Because of the dynamic nature of the Internet, any web addresses or links contained in this book may have changed since publication and may no longer be valid. The views expressed in this work are solely those of the author and do not necessarily reflect the views of the publisher, and the publisher hereby disclaims any responsibility for them.

Contents

Introduction vii
Chapter 1   Chevron Southern Platform (North Sea) 1
Chapter 2   Algiers (Algeria) 8
Chapter 3   Curacao (Netherlands Antilles) 24
Chapter 4   Esso Fawley (Southampton) 29
Chapter 5   Training Course (Bahamas) 33
Chapter 6   Mossmorran (Fife) 64
Chapter 7   Sacramento (United States) 71
Chapter 8   Darwin (Australia) 81

Introduction

This book is intended to help with and highlight the trials and tribulations facing all men and women, young and old, who work for multinational companies, travelling the world to either maintain or install their equipment and enhance their companies' reputations.

Using the word "prostitute" is in no way intended to be evocative of anyone who finds himself or herself using this means to enhance his or her monetary status or to gain valuable experience in his or her chosen profession.

The title may seem slightly harsh in describing a career with an established company one would think would cover all eventualities when an employee is travelling and working outside the assurances of the company's premises on their behalf.

An employee, after a short briefing in which he or she is told very little, on some occasions travels while hoping and praying that the fax or phone call that has requested his or her presence is genuine and that all arrangements for his or her arrival to his or her final destination have been approved by both client and company.

The events that generated your request to travel are subdued, and after leaving the mother company premises, you generally find you're on your own not only in travelling to your destination but also in looking for information and assistance before actually getting to the end destination.

As a traveller, I found myself one of these prostitutes, dragged about from pillar to post hoping and sometimes praying that when I had a bit of time to myself that the nightmare which had evolved would vanish and everything would return to normality. Lucky for me, this did happen, but it could have been a lot worse and may not have turned into a happy ending.

Multinational companies' employees who deal with people travelling do not have the proper knowledge or seek to acquire knowledge of the countries they send their fellow employees to. The travellers sometimes find themselves in a hostile environment, not properly prepared to handle what is ahead of them.

Most of the time, the employee who hands you the ticket for your journey is unaware about the situation he or she is sending you into. There is no discussion of things you should or should not do regarding the cultures of the people you are going to meet and work with.

When it came to countries that had a history of unrest or countries we hadn't done work in before, someone would generally phone up the home office and ask whether there were any restrictions on travel. Unless a war was on, the answer was the same: "We have no reason to believe that travelling is not safe." This covered them from a multitude of sins.

If you have to travel, you usually have to do your own investigation, and generally you don't have the time, as you have just arrived from another contract and wish to have a bit of quality time with your family. There is nothing worse than being called into the office during this time to do work that either the project manager or secretary could carry out on your behalf.

All the stories written in the book are real-life situations that I experienced. Some of them were caused by a lack of forward thinking in regard to proper research; others were caused by fellow employees who were entrenched in their own positions and did not care for the well-being of fellow travellers.

One of the most annoying things in the eighties and nineties was the length of time it took to get to most contracts. Sometimes three or four different plane journeys took up two days, and at the end of all this the traveller would have to go to work the next day and perform miracles.

During my travels, I was sent to Kuwait just before the Iraqi invasion. When senior managers were challenged about the situation, this was brushed aside. They emphasised that the foreign office had said that at this moment in time people were free to travel but should stay tuned to the news. No manager actually thought that if an invasion took place, all the expats working in that country could be evacuated. If there were an invasion, would the occupiers stop to let us all leave the country as if nothing had happened?

The invasion eventually took place and is now history. It led to Britain and America declaring war on Iraq to liberate Kuwait and bring back Kuwait independence.

From my point of view, this seemed more than just a bit careless; but as the money was paid up front by the client, there was no question. Someone had to go, and I was that unlucky person.

One of my many memories was watching on BBC News as a British Airways plane sitting on the runway, ready for take-off, was stopped by an Iraqi tank and all the passengers taken prisoner. My heart sank, because days earlier I had flown out on that same plane. I sat at home saying to myself, *How close was that?* The hostages were paraded about as if it were a great coup, but most of the people on board were just in the country to do jobs for their companies.

I would like to say that not all my travels were fraught with troubles; some stories are quite hilarious, as you will find out later in the book. But most of all these circumstances were brought about by not being properly prepared and arrangements not being detailed enough before and during my travels.

Chapter 1

CHEVRON SOUTHERN PLATFORM (NORTH SEA)

My first encounter with an international company as a travelling prostitute was when I worked in our factory test area. My manager came round and asked, "Would anyone like to go offshore for two weeks?" The remit was to stand by two Frame Size 5001 50 Hertz gas turbine–powered trains while handing over the maintenance contract to another contractor. It seemed quite straightforward, so I volunteered.

Reporting to the service department for a briefing, with them knowing this was my first time outside the company on this sort of activity, I was prepared for a lengthy meeting to go over drawings and procedural requirements. I was wrong.

Eager and apprehensive about what I had let myself in for, I was astounded that no drawings were produced and no procedural requirements were itemised. I was just handed a train ticket to Aberdeen, notified of the hotel I was to stay in overnight and told to turn up at Dyce Airport early in the morning. My instructions were to go to the helicopter departure area and present my travel documents, and that was it. Ten minutes.

Being inquisitive and cautious, and thinking, *It can't be as easy as this*, I carried out some research on the types of machines, sizes of machines, and types of auxiliary equipment I would encounter on the trip. From that information, I could find drawings and outstanding defects, which I should have been made aware of before going offshore.

So off I went, carrying my documentation, my change of clothes, and all other essentials I presumed were required.

I arrived at the helicopter area and presented my travel documents, and everything seemed okay – until I noticed everyone was dressed for Antarctic weather though this was the middle of summer. Realizing I was not properly dressed for this journey, I asked, "Is there a platform representative available to discuss this problem?" The answer was no, as it was seven o'clock in the morning. That was asking a little too much.

Sticking out like a sore thumb, I queued to board the helicopter, hurrying along because I wanted a window seat. It was my first visit offshore, and I wanted to see everything I could, because I might not get the chance to go offshore again.

After I was seated a couple of minutes later, the co-pilot made a point in coming over and welcoming me on board with kind words (first time offshore) and then walked away laughing this made me feel real good.

Travelling to the platform, it was not long before the necessity of the Antarctic clothing became evident. The helicopter was freezing. I was sitting there shivering for over an hour and feeling really pissed off and angry that the so-called briefing did not mention the fact that the helicopter would be freezing and really noisy.

Then the co-pilot appeared and read out the names of people who were disembarking at the central platform. To my surprise, my name was read. After he had finished, I shouted to him for his attention. He came over, and I explained that his information was incorrect and that I should disembark at the southern platform. I asked, "Can you radio ahead for verification?"

That was the wrong thing to do.

On arrival at the platform, the co-pilot appeared and started reading out the names of people who were to disembark, and unsurprisingly, my name was read out. So I just sat there not moving, as I knew that his information was wrong. With everyone else gone, he came across and said, "Off."

I explained again that I was expected on the other platform. He retorted, "Get *fucking* off, or I'll throw you off." This took me by total surprise. Not for one minute did I expect someone with his authority to speak to a passenger, never mind in that manner.

I got off and went downstairs to the purser's cabin. There I was met by a friendly gentleman. After I gave him my name, he checked his paperwork and, lo and behold, said, "You should not be here. You were to have gone to the southern platform."

I explained what had happened, and to my surprise, he said, "You can't talk back to the helicopter crew. These people are *gods* and will not listen to you." That was something else that would have been useful to know at the meeting.

The purser then said, "Don't worry. We have a mail helicopter that travels between platforms and that will be leaving in a couple of hours. I'll get you on it."

He took me to the canteen for a bite to eat and then took me to the cinema room to watch a film. As he left, he said, "When the mail helicopter is ready to leave, I'll come and get you."

This small helicopter delivered technical documents as well as mail between the platforms – mostly technical details. What they never told me was that the pilot was a Vietnam War veteran and was quite mad.

After one hour – which was a waste of time, since I didn't see the beginning or the ending of the film – I was finally summoned to the purser's office. The helicopter was ready to leave.

I was taken up to the deck. The copter door opened, and I jumped in. With one glance by the pilot at my clothing, it was clear what he was thinking. Then he said the words I cringed at, First time off-shore (As if he didn't know).

"Yes," was the obvious reply? Very softly I heard him say, "Good." Just before I got a chance to ask him what he had said, he started the noisy engine, handing me a set of ear defenders to dampen down the noise. I'm sure he held them back just so I could be deafened by the engine noise.

Hovering slightly above the helicopter pad, he jumped off the platform, nose diving towards the sea. This caused me to slightly shit my pants, which he seemed to take great pleasure from. In seeing me go chalk white, he seemed to act more brazen. Throwing the little helicopter about seemed to give him more fun than he had had for many years. Doing the same job must have been boring to him.

For myself, worse was to come.

As the pilot looked at me and laughed, his concentration was not what it should have been. He overshot the first staging post – the northern platform – if you could call it that. It was still under construction and only a shadow of the platform I had left. This was Chevron's third platform in this section of the North Sea. So it was my turn to smile as he went chalk white, but it was a wry smile, as I was still at his mercy.

After leaving the northern platform, it took only ten minutes to arrive at my destination, the southern platform, so you can imagine that leaving the helicopter was a relief beyond belief.

After arriving at my destination, I was shown to my accommodation by the purser. He asked how I'd enjoyed the mail helicopter ride and found it quite amusing when I said I did not.

The lodgings were good. There were two two-man bunk beds, and as I entered, right at the back of me was one of my room-mates. He introduced himself and explained that he was a North Sea veteran along with his two mates, whom I would meet quite soon.

My new friend's next statement was, "Top bunk," as the bottom bunks had been taken.

"It's nice to meet you too," I uttered.

As the platform was having maintenance carried out, it was fully manned with maintenance personnel. The only cabin that had a bunk available was one that was occupied by three roughnecks, and this was to be mine for next three days. The roughnecks were all right, but they were very rough; their language was not totally refined – not that it had to be – but they were good, and some of their patter was quite hilarious. My biggest fear came when they stopped talking and the lights went out. I thought I was in a war zone with the noise that came from each bunk.

On the first day, I went through a survival-introduction course shown round the platform, which was just as imagined, only bigger. And I had something to eat. This was not what I expected. The food that was served up was unbelievable. The selection was certainly too much for me; and it was far too much for most of workers, because the waste was terrible. I watched men load up their plates with food, only to take a few bits and throw the rest in the waste bin. It was not pleasant to watch and to crown it all, they went back and took another full plate of food and through some of that away. This was totally different from my upbringing, when you would not be allowed to leave the table until your plate was clean, and if there was any extra, it was a bonus. Moving on, I watched half a film and turned in, expecting to meet the chief engineer the next day for a rough introduction into my duties for the next two weeks.

Wrong.

After breakfast the next morning, fitted out with North Sea overalls and boots, I met the chief engineer and was told in no uncertain manner that my company had been a disgrace. The performance of our engineers had caused problems, and if I didn't know what I was doing, I should leave everything alone and just sit and wait till the new people arrived in one week. This was not the greeting I expected. I was taken aback by the ferocity of the attack.

Without causing a scene, I sat back and listened to the complaints, as they were nothing to do with me. After he finished, I explained my background and explained that as I had only a week before the handover, I should start work immediately to try to solve some of the problems.

The verbal attack from the chief engineer was the first of its kind; as my experiences developed, a few similar instances occurred.

I asked to see the defect log and the previous site reports from my predecessors. It was quite obvious there were issues to be attended to, mostly due to calibration of the equipment. After reviewing the data presented to me, I spent most of day devising a workable program, bearing in mind the time factor.

I contacted the chief engineer with a proposal to eliminate most of the problems. This meant shutting down the machines one at a time and doing a complete calibration of the control parts, which I had identified as a major contributor to the problems experienced.

I produced a program the chief engineer reviewed with me and his technicians, and my proposal was scrutinised intensely before I was given the go-ahead for just one machine – the one that was giving the most problems.

Over the next two days, the work was carried out. The full calibration required adjustments to suit the running conditions, and as this was the worst performing machine, some instrumentation from the field had to be replaced. The unit was then put online and performed satisfactorily.

Over the coming four days, the remaining work on the program was carried out. The units were shut down one by one and successfully put back online to the satisfaction of the chief engineer.

So what was meant to be an easy two-week trip offshore ended up being six days of non-stop fourteen-hour-a-day hard graft. With the rig's personnel scrutinising every change I made, it was not a nice feeling.

When I thought all was good and was ready to relax, on came the new company's representative – an American. He informed me that part and parcel of handover activity was to go through a complete installation calibration on all machines before final handover. This had been agreed upon with my office months prior – another thing they apparently forgot to inform me about.

The other thing that he informed me of was that he had never worked on this type of machine before. I informed him that the chief engineer was not keen on people that didn't know what they were doing, and I advised him to pay attention to what I would be showing him and not to tell anyone what he had just said to me.

Here I was, training this man and handing over a contract to another company – a contract which my company lost because we didn't supply the correct men to fulfil the client's needs. And the company that had taken over the contract had sent someone that didn't know too much about the job. Our performance must have been really bad.

One incident that was quite amusing took place in the canteen. As I said earlier, there was everything and more; there was even an ice cream machine. When you see two grown men standing toe to toe over who gets the last ice cream, then you know you have been offshore too long. And that's exactly what happened. There was quite a large queue for the ice cream, and someone standing in the queue started talking to a colleague who joined him halfway along. As they continued talking, they got closer to the ice cream machine. When they eventually got there, the two men each took a cone, and there seemed to be no problem. But it just so happened that they got the last cones, and the machine ran out of ice cream. The man who was next in the queue blew up and insisted that the guy who had joined the queue halfway down should hand over his cone to him, and hence an impasse was reached. It was not a pleasant sight; it got so bad, in fact, that the two men were reprimanded.

After completing all the obligations of my company, I left the North Sea platform with a final endorsement from the chief engineer that if I ever wanted to come offshore, there was a job there for me. That gave me great satisfaction, as he didn't know how apprehensive I was about not working on a whole installation with all the auxiliary equipment and an alternator coupled to the machine. This was a first for me, and with his first comments about the men who had been here before ringing in my ears, I had been concerned that I could have been thrown off the platform.

Knowing that I had carried out my duties correctly even though the people in charge of my well-being did not do theirs very satisfactorily gave me great pride.

As you might imagine, upon returning to the office I had numerous points to bring up at the debriefing, which one would automatically take for granted would be carried out. Wrong. No one was available. I was told the following: "Send an email of your concerns, and thanks for a job well done! If you would like to join the Service Department, then there's a senior position here for you."

I returned to the Test Department, and it was over two years before I finally became a permanent travelling prostitute.

Joining the Service Department was not an easy choice to make. Leaving my family when I went travelling was very hard; the goal was to achieve stability in home life. The major reason for my choice was a recession which was causing a lack of orders for new machines in the factory. Redundancies were inevitable. So travelling was not my first choice, but it did secure my employment.

The errors and lack of understanding of the pressures and difficulties experienced offshore and travelling in general were still fresh in my mind. I was very surprised, even shocked, that not one of them was addressed. Assurances which were given were broken from assignment to assignment, as my further experience showed.

The good thing about my experience travelling to the North Sea was that it taught me to take nothing for granted and try to cover all eventualities that I could think of before setting off on a journey.

Chapter 2

ALGIERS (ALGERIA)

Upon joining the Service Division, my first assignment was a service installation in Algiers. The machines on site were a Frame-Size MS5001 50 Hertz generator set which I was going to commission. One had been stripped down and was in the process of being put back together. This trip was to take no more than three weeks.

After my last experience, I compiled a list of questions relating to what may or may not arise before I arrived on site:

1. Transportation flight details
2. Accommodation hotel location
3. Site visiting (address details)
4. Site location (coastal, inland)
5. Point of contact (client's supervisor)
6. Temperature (daytime, night-time)
7. Purpose of visit (any drawings available, any site passes required, any major defects)
8. Restrictions in the country (visas, required documentation)
9. Medical facilities
10. Injections required
11. Work instructions (scope of supply)
12. Contact at airport

After asking questions regarding all these points, I presumed that everything was covered. All points were addressed, and I was looking forward to a trouble-free trip. How wrong I was.

Before I left the office, the manager called me in to his office not to give me further advice about the contract but to inform me that whisky is very expensive in Algiers and, as the men had been working on site now for two months, they would appreciate if I could bring in a couple of bottles and put the cost through on expenses when I got home.

It seemed a fair request, so I put it in the memory bank to allow a little extra time at the duty free.

Arriving at Glasgow Airport Sunday morning, I was met by a letter at the check-in desk instructing me that freight had been assigned to the aircraft under my name. The packages were for site installation. An advice note enclosed listed the total cost of packages as zero – free of charge.

This was to ensure that customs at the other end did not charge duty on the items. This set me back. Everything was calculated till the letter appeared – especially at the last minute. As I was checking in, it was brought to my attention that the freight documentation had not been completed correctly, so I had to look through my documentation for dates, site names, purposes of use, and end users' addresses. This seemed to take ages. After clearing up all the points reading the documentation – for turbine bearings (I didn't understand how these could be claimed as hand freight) – it was time to get to the departure terminal. The time for boarding the plane was upon me.

Having not a lot of time, I ended up running to the duty free to purchase two bottles of whisky before going to the departure lounge, which I did just in time (another example of office staff not notifying the people or person travelling of the correct information).

Sitting on the flight, I reviewed the letter for further information so that when I went through customs in Algeria I knew exactly what I was carrying. The letter said the freight was two pairs of turbine bearings. The type of bearings was not important, as no information was given. It did say that I would be met at the airport by the client's representative. He would take the items to the site, and they would be available the next morning for site installation.

I arrived in Algeria. Before going to customs, I was very aware of the notice boards around the arrival hall explaining that no alcoholic spirits could be taken into the country. Here I was carrying two bottles of spirits on the instruction of a senior manager, who I would have thought would have known that no alcohol was allowed in the country. To put someone new in this position was the height of incompetence.

Algeria's drink laws presented me with my first dilemma: how to get rid of the two bottles of spirits I bought at the duty free shop. I looked around the arrival hall for somewhere to dump my cargo, but there was no place to put them. I presumed customs would confiscate them without any fuss at the customs desk. This was a genuine mistake on my behalf.

On arriving at the carousel to collect my case and the extra baggage, what a fright I faced. These were not small parcels containing one item; these parcels contained the whole bearings. These were the main bearings of a gas turbine, and they were so heavy I could not lift them off the revolving carousel. Eventually I dragged the bearings onto a low-lying trolley supplied by one of the airport staff, which I was very thankful for, and made my way to the customs area, where I was to be met by the client's representative and one of my colleagues. While I was waiting, a fellow passenger faced my dilemma about duty free alcohol. Rather than simply confiscating the drink, they insisted on him emptying all his belongings out and removing his shoes; he stripped down to practically nothing. My stomach sank, as I knew this was going to happen to me.

After waiting till I was nearly the last in the arrival hall, and still hoping that someone from the client side or one of my colleagues would come and make contact so that the drink situation plus all the bearing problems could be resolved, no one was to be seen.

I was on my own. I was called forward by the customs officer and asked if I had anything to declare. I produced the invoice supplied by my office. He reviewed the invoice and asked to see the items. The customs officer was three feet off the ground, and as he could not see the items, he asked me to lift them up onto the desk next to him, which I could not do. Seeing that I was struggling, he called over the soldier who was checking the passengers, and he then started pointing his gun at me, demanding I lift the items onto to the desk. I then had to explain to him that I could not, as they were very heavy.

Trials and Tribulations of a Travelling Prostitute

Eventually, when I was the last person in the airport apart for security and airport staff, the customs officer came round and opened up the crate to check the bearings. He called over his supervisor for a second opinion.

They said that the paperwork was not correct, and he had to impound the goods till further inspection in the morning. This was music to my ears, as there was no way I could get the parcels into a taxi and then at the other end get them back out and into the hotel. They gave me a telephone number which I was to call. They told me they would inform me when the goods would be inspected, and I or our client's representative would have to be present if we wanted them cleared to enter Algeria.

After this long, drawn-out affair over the extra freight, they turned their attention to my personal belongings, insisting on opening my case. This they did, going through every item. I deliberately hid my hand case from the customs officer's vision. He stamped my papers, and I was allowed to leave.

I quite believe they were just glad to get rid of me, as it was Sunday night and very late.

Leaving the airport, I was still hoping someone would arrive to pick me up and take me to the hotel. No chance.

Lucky for me, if you can call it lucky, a taxi driver witnessed my deliberations at customs and stayed behind when everyone else had left, hoping I would require a lift. And he was right. I showed him the hotel and address. He agreed to take me there, and then he left me and went for his car. At first I thought he was leaving me standing. As it was late and the hotel was over an hour away, I was expecting the worst, so you can imagine my relief when, just as I was giving up, he appeared. I was thankful, saying to myself, "This is one taxi driver which will get a very good tip."

On the other hand, here I was, alone outside an international airport, with no one around other than one taxi driver whom I had to depend on to get me to a hotel miles outside Algiers. He could have taken me anywhere, robbed me, or even killed me, and no one would have known what had happened – all because my travel arrangements had not been sent to the appropriate people or the appropriate people didn't have the decency to read the information and pick me up at the airport.

On arriving at the hotel, he informed me that the fare was ten thousand dinars I told him to wait here as I needed to cash a sterling traveller's cheque to obtain dinars so that I could pay him. He informed me he would cash it for me. Being aware that all foreign currency had to be receipted and would be inspected when leaving the country, I asked him if he had an official stamp. He replied no, so I informed him that I would prefer that the hotel change the currency and started to walk away towards the hotel reception.

The taxi driver became a bit angry and said he wanted me to pay in pounds. He told me that if I did not, he would drive away with my cases in his boot. I asked how much he wanted in pounds, and fifty pounds was his reply. I had only forty pounds in cash and explained I would have to cash in a traveller's cheque if he did not accept the forty pounds. He did accept the money, retrieved my cases from the boot, and drove away.

To be quite honest, I would have paid him double the fee if I had more cash on me. This left me feeling a little vexed, as I appreciated that the Algerian currency was quite weak and he deserved better.

After checking in at reception, I was directed to one of the upper levels – the same level my fellow employees were residing on. I obtained their room numbers and decided that after I settled in to my room, I would give them a call and find out about the arrangements in the morning.

The room was very basic, with a bed, one cupboard, one mirror, very high ceilings, and a toilet. To be quite honest, it was not very appealing. I dropped my cases and just fell onto the bed, shut my eyes, and said to myself, "That was a horrendous experience. Wait till I meet my fellow employees; they will get a piece of my mind for not meeting me at the airport."

After a couple of minutes, I opened my eyes, and lo and behold, there was a lizard right above my head. I am sure I shit myself. I phoned reception, and they assured me that it was not a concern. In fact, they assured me that if any mosquitoes came into the room, the *Gecko* would get them before they could bite me. "Wonderful," I said to myself, "they even gave their lizard a name." I did not know at the time that "Gecko" is, I believe, French for "small lizard". I then hung up.

I phoned my workmates. They were all assembled in one room. *Good*, I thought. *Having them in one room means that I will not have to repeat myself three times when I'm lambasting them for leaving me stranded.*

I knocked on the room door, and the younger of my three fellow employees opened the door. His first words, which I believe were rehearsed, were "What are you doing here? You are not expected till tomorrow night." I asked him to look at the last email sent to the hotel on Friday, look at the date, and then look at today's date. Then the half-hearted apologies were given.

As I walked into the room, the first thing which stuck out like a sore thumb was crates of empty wine bottles – hundreds of them – were stacked against the walls. It appeared that as whisky and other spirits were banned or too expensive on the black market, wines were the alternative, and this had become my colleagues' substitute.

There was obviously plenty of reasonably priced wine. I asked why all the empty bottles were still there, and they told me that the cleaners would not remove any wine bottles from the room.

Still foaming at the airport fiasco I asked what time we were to leave the hotel in the morning. Smelling alcohol on their breath, I decided that it was not worth my while complaining about being left high and dry at the airport, so I started to leave. Their parting words were "Six thirty." As I left the room, my parting words to them were "See you for breakfast at 6.30 am. If you all can all make it on time and it's not too much bother."

Before I left the room, one of the mechanical supervisors – who, in my opinion, was drunk – shouted, "Did you bring a bottle?"

Not answering, I went to my room and unpacked.

I mentioned earlier that the room was very basic. After examining a little more I came to the conclusion that it was less than basic. The lighting was dim, and the bathroom was in a poor state, so I decided to pull out my work clothes, leave them hanging on the wardrobe, and leave the rest of my clothes in the case along with the clothes I had arrived in.

As it was very late, I turned in. My lizard friend was busy darting about. I pulled the sheet over my head and tried to get some sleep.

I arose at first light. Taking out my toiletries, I preceded to the toilet, hoping that there would be running water. To my surprise, there was; but no hot water was available. I just washed the main parts and headed for breakfast.

When I arrived for breakfast, to my surprise, all three fellow employees were already there and had ordered. Once again, this was not the place to get full English. An omelette was on the menu, and no one would vary from that, as the chefs were a little short on European culinary cuisine.

Conversation about the hotel's condition led to discussion about the fact that this was the best in the area. My first reply was "Where else have you tried?" As we were over an hour and half away from the site, I thought surely there must have been a place closer with the same exotic decor. I quit the subject believing that we were there only because it suited the two senior men's drinking habits.

It was explained to me that the hotel complex was constructed when the French were in control of Algeria and that it was one of the main holiday attractions. Since they left, it had been in steady decline, along with a lot of the infrastructure there. Bear in mind that when the French left, they took or destroyed all the plans in Algeria.

Knowing that I had to work with these guys for a couple of weeks, I backed off and started talking about the job itself. It was soon apparent that the three weeks I had been told the trip was going to take would be more like six weeks. In fact, it took eleven weeks. This was a shocker. The thought of staying with these guys for this length of time was quite frightening, as I could not see myself working and socializing with these men – who were drunks in my eyes at this time – for this length of time.

The omelette was not that bad, but I was told, "That's it; you'll have the same every morning."

Not a problem, I thought. *Six weeks of that – I'll survive.* But I was sick of omelettes by the time I actually left.

When we left the hotel, our driver was waiting. He introduced himself as Abdul. We started out along the coast road to Algiers. It was not a bad road, but the driving was sometimes a bit iffy. When we got to Algiers itself, he became quite mad, taking chances which were totally dangerous. When none of my colleagues sat in the front seat, I'd thought they were being gentlemen. I should have known better. I was totally shit-scared at the driving, and eventually I shut my eyes and braced myself for a crash. My colleagues were wetting themselves at my expressions. It must have been funny for them, and thinking about it after the event, it was funny. And to be fair to the driver, if he had not driven the way he did, we would probably have ended up in a smash, as the other drivers were driving just as badly if not worse. Every manoeuvre that was carried out was followed by a loud blast of the horn. You can imagine how glad I was when we arrived at the site a bit deaf but all in one piece.

The first hour after arriving on site was set aside for meeting site personnel. This was very brief, and it was plainly obvious that there was a bit of hostility between the site superintendent and our engineers, which proved to be quite obstructive during my visit.

My next task was to contact the site agent and let him know that the bearings had been impounded at the airport and we should retrieve them as soon as possible. Based on my experience at the airport, if the goods were not identified and retrieved quickly, they would probably be stolen or damaged if left at the airport, so it was imperative that we get to the airport as soon as possible. He appreciated what I said and told me he would be there as soon as possible.

Our agent arrived in the afternoon, and off we went to the airport. Just as I thought, after just this short period of time, all the parcels were broken open and the bearings had been left scattered over the holding area's floor. The agent produced more paperwork for the customs men, but still this was not enough and we left empty-handed. The bearings didn't get to the site till the Friday.

On the documents I received, the reason for sending the bearings out with me as hand baggage was that they were needed on site immediately. It took three weeks, to be precise.

It did appear that the messages sent from the site to the company office were far from the truth, and the schedule stated was a fantasy. There was no way that this could possibly be met. The site was covering up a lack of progress; as a consequence, it appeared that my time on site was going to be a lot longer than I had originally planned.

If the hotel was basic, then the site amenities were even more basic. Nothing was available. We had to go out and buy coffee, tea, and bread rolls from a baker up a side street and avoid particles of dust and everything else being shaken from bedding and clothing onto the street from every balcony.

When I opened up the control panel for the first time, I was quite surprised that the panel interior was clean and everything was in place. This came as quite a shock, considering the age of the equipment. While browsing the panel, I felt the presence of someone. I turned round to find the site manager standing at my back. I hadn't heard him enter the cab, and I got quite a fright, maybe because all that I had gone through the first day and night, plus the driver's exhibition on the roads, made me very jumpy.

I gave him credit for keeping the panel in good condition. We talked about his schedule, and he was concerned that the time was passing and they required the machine as soon as possible. He then said, "When are you powering up the panel?" I replied, "As soon as I carry out the following checks." I handed him a typical installation procedure that detailed all the wiring, earthing, and card checks.

He seemed quite agitated and said, "There is nothing wrong with the panel."

I retorted by saying, "That's fine; then the checks will be straightforward and we can move on to all the field devices which have been removed for the major overhaul."

He abruptly left, and I was standing there thinking, *Did I say something wrong, or was it my breath?* Whatever it was, it was not very nice of him to leave like that. But as the trip and work progressed, the reason for his behaviour became apparent.

Travelling back to the hotel, it was apparent that the journey to the site in the morning was not reckless just because the roads were busy; it was because the driver was crazy. Again we were subjected to a journey mixed with near misses, horns blasting, and severe braking. And to crown it all, a couple of days later, outside of Algiers, there were lovely orange orchards along the main road. The driver asked if we would like to taste the oranges. Yes was the overwhelming reply. I expected him to turn off the road, look for a farmer, and ask to buy some. But no, he just swung off the road and into the middle of the field, jumped onto the roof of the car, and started throwing the oranges into the car. Three farmers ran into the field and confronted the driver. He eventually gave back the oranges, and we were allowed to leave.

That we left the orchard by the correct way was a surprise in its own right. But before we got to the exit, our driver again stopped the car, jumped onto the roof, threw four oranges into the cab, and made off as fast as he could.

Trials and Tribulations of a Travelling Prostitute

Once back at the hotel, I confronted my colleagues about the driver. They told me other drivers were worse, though I found this hard to believe. Maybe the driver's behaviour was the reason why they drank so much.

As you will remember, I had been instructed by my senior manager to bring to the site a couple of bottles of whisky so that the site personnel could enjoy a wee dram – a luxury they had been deprived of since arriving in Algeria. They certainly had been deprived of a wee dram, but not alcohol, since coming to the site.

It had been an endeavour to escape customs with the whisky intact, and now I was faced with the problem of when to hand it over. As I am not a whisky drinker myself, it was no good to me, but I knew that handing over whisky to two of my three colleagues could and probably would be a disaster. I decided that it would wise to hand it over at the weekend if we were not working on the next day. This, I believed, would be the safest course of action.

That evening, while sitting in my room with my new friend the lizard, writing my log, I was taken aback by a knock on the door. It was the youngest member of my three colleagues. He asked if he could come in, and I said, "Of course." He then sat down and spouted out what it had been like working here for the last six weeks, sometimes crying. It was a catalogue of abuse.

As he had just joined the company straight from university, my two senior personnel seemed to be taking great pleasure in making life hell for the trainee. He then informed me that he was to work alongside me in the commissioning phase of the overhaul – another thing office personnel forgot to tell me before I left for the site. After spouting out his anxieties and his fears, he seemed to relax. It's amazing; sometimes you need someone to talk to just to express your feelings and relieve all the tension that builds up inside. This seemed to be just the trick for my colleague.

It was agreed the next day that the trainee would work alongside me. But if he was required on the rebuild of the machine, he would work with the mechanical engineers. I would keep notes on everything I was doing so he could follow my progress. This was not a problem, as I would be doing so anyhow.

After a couple of weeks, the student informed me that if I had not come out, he might have cracked up and demanded to be sent home even if it meant being sacked. I tried to keep him calm, which sometimes was not easy, and kept him away from the two senior engineers as much as I possibly could. We managed to get along, and the days were getting better. I did not want tell him that without him there, I probably would have cracked up also.

One week later, on a Saturday, my two colleagues, on leaving the site quite late, asked the driver where we could purchase more wine. The driver informed them that it would be quite difficult given the time and because it was a holiday for the locals. They insisted, telling him there must be some place. Again the driver said it would be very difficult. The only place he knew of was miles from our location and was in a housing scheme which was not too friendly to non-Algerians. They said not to worry, as they would not leave the car.

I tried to persuade them not to go looking for this place and get us back to the hotel, where we might get some wine from the hotel staff. "No chance" was the reply; my request and my wishes fell on deaf ears, and off we went, looking for a place to buy wine, not knowing what to expect.

After driving for about fifteen minutes up a quite steep hill from which we saw a wonderful view of Algiers, which was quite impressive, we turned off the main road and entered a built-up area. Lots and lots of cars were parked along both sides of the narrow road. Our speed was reduced to twenty miles an hour – and even slower when we came to T-junctions and bends. Quite a few people were staring at our car, and I was feeling quite uncomfortable I said to the driver, "How long do we have to travel in this area?"

"Not long" was the reply.

Round the next bend, as the driver has said, we saw a shop in the distance. Just when we were slowing down, we hit another car. Panic set in. *What do we do?* My first reaction was to get away from here and come back tomorrow and see if we can find the owner and clear it up. Within minutes, people were gathering. They were staring into the car, pointing in our direction. The driver was trying to explain to the people, but as he was speaking in Arabic, we did not know what he was saying.

After sitting in the car for some time, getting more worried by the minute, the driver started the car up and drove through the crowd and shot away. No wine was bought. The trip was a total waste of time that

Trials and Tribulations of a Travelling Prostitute

could have ended with more serious consequences. I could sense the relief in everyone. Even my two colleagues admitted it had been a big mistake. Without speaking too much, we had something to eat and went to our rooms.

The next weekend, we had Friday and Saturday off because of a religious holiday. This was the ideal time to produce the whisky. This I did, and we had a celebration in one of the rooms after they called me a few choice names for holding on to it for such a long time. They made short work of it.

If I had had any foresight into what they told the senior manager when they arrived back at the office, I would have poured the whisky down the drain. They informed him in turn that they were teetotal until I brought out the whisky and that things went downhill after that. All the empty bottles of wine in their rooms must have arrived there empty. This is what I was faced with when I came home. Not only did I have to clear up the mess they left at the site, but I also had to answer to a charge which was outrageous and stupid for my manger to suggest.

During the holiday weekend, a local waiter gave us directions to a restaurant which had a good name for seafood cuisine. This was a prayer answered – something different to eat – so we ordered a taxi and went along. Before going into the restaurant, we went to a local bar and ordered a couple of beers. We sat talking generally about the job and a million other things. I crossed my legs just to be more comfortable, unintentionally showing the sole of my shoe to a local. The next minute, the local took umbrage at this and began shouting and bawling in my direction. We, along with the owner, tried to calm him down by apologising and offering to buy him a drink. The owner and his staff in the bar calmed the situation. Just when we thought everything was taken care of, more locals got involved. The owner explained that as a local custom, you never show the sole of your shoe, as it indicates that the person who sees it is beneath you. We left the bar quickly; the restaurant was not far along the road.

As the waiter had said, it was clean and had a reasonable menu. We all ordered, and three out of the four of us ordered the fish of the day – a bad mistake. As it was a holiday, the fish must have been lying out for a few days, and once I ate a piece, my stomach told me it was off. I informed the rest of the crew, and they passed the fish by. After eating the fish, I had diarrhea for six days. I took Lomotil an anti-diarrhea tablets, which were given out by the company to stop upset stomachs. I was eating them like sweeties. The stomach cramps just would not stop. Eventually I was on the verge of going home, as I was losing too much weight.

Just when I was about to pack my bags the stomach pains stopped. After eating very little and drinking plenty over the next week or so, I was back to my normal self. The experience was not nice. When travelling, make sure you have the right medication.

During the commissioning, I discovered why the site manager wanted me to power up the panel immediately when I arrived on site. He had removed working cards from the control panel and replaced them with ones that had failed, hoping that when I powered up the panel, he could claim that I damaged the cards and charge my company for new cards. It was nasty work, but this gives you an idea of how the relationship between my colleagues and the client had broken down long before I arrived.

I made a list of the faulty cards and informed the site manger that this machine could not have run with these damaged cards. He took them away and produced new cards, which were probably the original ones, and I moved on.

Once the unit had been reassembled, the head office replaced my two mechanical colleagues. One left because of a bereavement, and the other left to go to a new contract.

Before we put the unit on line, we were notified that a senior mechanical engineer would be coming to the site to check over the installation at the request of the client, as he did not have any confidence in the mechanical installation that my two compatriots carried out.

As the client had concern about the mechanical installation and the extra time taken on site, I assumed the man they sent out would be one of their very best, bearing in mind that one of the service's unwritten laws was to keep the client happy at all times.

He arrived on site and explained that he was a bit rusty at this stage in the proceedings. That's the last thing I wanted to hear. My first thoughts were about what the client was going to say; he was expecting a senior man to ensure him that everything was done correctly and we were all ready to go.

I must admit that he surprised me as he thoroughly went about inspecting all the data settings and procedures with great care and expertise, including the client in his assessment and the work he was carrying out, and showing the client all the data. He was happy to proceed.

I presume he had made his statement about being a bit rusty just to cover himself till he saw all the data.

He asked me if there was anything he could do to assist with the commissioning. I showed him the turbine starting means, which was a diesel engine, showed him the schematic, and asked him to fill the system with diesel oil to prepare for firing.

While he was doing that, I finished of the calibration of the fire protection system. This took me about two hours. I was surprised my new colleague did not come back looking for something else to do, so I went outside to see what was happening, and there he was, still filling up the diesel engine. I showed him the schematic and explained that the bypass pipe was taking all the fuel he was putting in back to the tank. Sometimes you have to shake your head in despair and move on. I believe that is what he meant when he said he was a bit rusty; hands-on commission was not his field.

After firing up the unit for the first time, everything went like clockwork until we started generating power above ten megawatts. The curves showed it was generating just slightly less than expected with the ambient temperature in the afternoon. The recorded data showed we had a higher-than-expected vibration and temperature within either the gearbox or the generator bearings; that's what the electronic sensors were telling me. Instead of letting the unit run at that load to see if the vibration would come down, the site manager insisted on us running at full power. I explained to him that all the bearings inside the turbine, gearbox, and generator were all new and had to be run in, just like the engine of a new auto. I kept the machine running for thirty minutes, and within that time I carried on doing final calibration adjustments on speed and temperature control.

Going back to the vibration system, I checked the sensor signals, which were all correct. Even at the reduced load, the values, if anything, had started to creep slightly up, which was concerning.

The client appeared after thirty minutes and insisted on taking the unit to maximum load. We did this, and the unit tripped. Yes, you guessed it – high vibrations.

I calibrated the entire vibration control system yet again, not finding any errors, and replaced vibration sensors for new ones at the request of the site manager. We fired up again, and yet again the unit tripped at the same load on high vibration.

The site manager called a meeting. The senior mechanical engineer and I went along, armed with our suggestion on the next step forward. Before we proposed our suggestion, the site manager produced a diary that contained entries detailing all the work carried out. Also in the diary were entries for all major procedures. Another thing in his diary was whether alcohol was present on our engineers' breath.

His diary showed that when alignment of the generator to gearbox was carried out, alcohol had been detected on the breath of my two colleagues.

The site supervisor insisted that a new alignment was required. This was not backed up by our data, and we put it to the meeting that if the alignment were out, then high vibration would be higher at full speed, no load, and half load, and this was not happening. As we were getting nowhere we suggested bringing in a local outside vibration expert at our cost. If, as we had said, the problem was not alignment, then the client would pay. This was agreed upon. To verify the type of vibration, the client was to select which company to carry out the tests. This was done, and the vibration was traced to the generator itself. The client had cleaned the windings with a solvent not approved by us or the generator manufacturer.

By using the solvent to clean the windings, they had removed some of the protective shellac. The removal of the shellac from the insulation applied to the windings in the factory causes the windings to expand more than allowed, causing an increase in temperature with an increase in load, and hence the increase in vibration.

I would like to say that the client's diary was damning, as there was a smell of alcohol on the breath of the engineers most of time when they could get wine, but they were not drunk by any stretch of the imagination. Hungover perhaps, slightly, but not drunk by any means. If the vibration survey carried out by the independent company had shown alignment was the problem, this would have been damning evidence and would have cost the company many thousands of pounds.

Leaving the site a relieved man, I swore, after all that had occurred, that if they sent me out to another site before Christmas with the same two employees, I would resign.

I arrived back at the head office, armed with all the data and a report, expecting some form of debriefing with senior management. Surprise, surprise – no one was available. "Please log your report and have a good Christmas," said my office contact.

This response annoyed me more this time than the other time simply because this time my safety had been put on the line. Two individuals had not had the decency to pick me up at the airport on Sunday night, a colleague had been abused to the state of nearly having a nervous breakdown, and I was blamed for turning two genuine religious non-alcoholics into alcoholics.

As it was coming up to Christmas, all the people I wanted to speak to were unavailable and on leave; so there I was, frustrated and angry, with no one to vent my anger to.

After the holidays, all my anger and frustration seemed to vanish as I realised it would have done no good ranting and raving about the visit, as it seemed that the whole office demeanour was one of not giving a shit.

It was becoming clearer that when I was out on site, no one in the office cared, and looking for answers to problems was a total waste of time.

Chapter 3

CURACAO (NETHERLANDS ANTILLES)

As I said in my introduction, not all visits were bad. This one was unbelievably good.

Curacao is located in the Caribbean, off the Venezuelan coast. We received an order for one Frame Size 5001 50 Hertz power generator set in 1979 and installed it in 1980–1981, and this was its first major overhaul, in 1983. The location of the installation was on the coast, inside a desalination plant.

Before going, I was informed that the plant's location could not have been in a better position on this beautiful Caribbean Island with a wonderful climate and with wonderful, friendly people.

Travelling out, the journey was as smooth as it possibly could have been – as it should be on all journeys. Everything went according to schedule. My flights were on time. I was met by a fellow employee at the airport and travelled to the hotel. I checked in and found I had a perfect room looking out onto quite a large swimming pool. I had something to eat and went to a local bar for a few beers. There my colleague and I met some of the local prostitutes, who were trying to secure some business. After we rejected an invitation to spend all night with Lucy for one hundred dollars, they soon lost interest in us and moved on, hoping for a more positive response. After an hour or so, we finished our drinks, and I retired to my room for the evening. It was a perfect start to a most enjoyable stay.

As the only plane I could take flew out on Saturday and arrived on Saturday, I had all Sunday to look at all the things required for Monday.

Working this way did not take too long, as the temperature was about 29 degrees Celsius with clear blue skies. This was perfect lounging-about-the pool weather, so with my bathing suit on, towel and sun cream at the ready, off I went. I found a nice position at the poolside and just lazed about all day. This was my type of overseas travel.

The next morning, it appeared that I had overdone the sunbathing, as my shoulders and the backs of the legs were more than a little burnt. Some after sun I bought at reception seemed to ease the pain slightly. As I had come from a climate of around zero degrees over Christmas, I should have known better. I never really knew exactly what kind of hours and what schedule I had to meet till it was spelled out to me the next morning by the client. The opportunity to relax and do a bit of sunbathing was not to be sniffed at, so the pain I was suffering at that time would ease and it would all be worthwhile.

Breakfast was good – a fine selection – and we travelled to the site. My remit was to check all electrical instrumentations and calibrate the control panel. This was standard procedure after a major overhaul. My colleague had already briefed me that there would be a delay to the original schedule.

Arriving on site, I was met by an electrical superintendent. He explained that the schedule was running slightly late, and as this was a lovely part of the world, he didn't think this would be any problem. I did not know too much of the place, but judging by what I had seen so far, staying an extra period of time would not cause me too much heartache.

Discussing what was required, he explained that the technicians under his control did not have lot of knowledge of power plant equipment and asked me if I could train a number of his technicians at the same time as doing my own work. I agreed to his request. I explained that most of my work would be located in the control cab for the first couple of weeks if everything went well, so the space would restrict the numbers. We agreed that only three technicians would work alongside me at any one time.

He also explained that the technicians would not be available till tomorrow. "Just have a browse about today, and you can start tomorrow. As it appears you seem to have had a little too much sun yesterday, the extra day off will assist your healing." He smiled. From that statement, I knew this was the kind of site manager I was going to get along with.

As the first week went by, it was plainly obvious that the reason for the work falling behind was the actual pace the local engineers worked at. It also appeared that in this part of the world, probably due to the heat, the engineers performed slowly and everyone seemed to go at a very slow pace. I assumed the couple of extra days would turn out to be more like a couple of weeks.

Not to upset anyone, as they were all very nice and gave me no grief, I slowed down my work to their pace and just moved along.

After four and a half weeks, all the calibration training was complete, and the electrical and instrumentation part was also complete. I was ready to fire up the unit. My colleague had a few mechanical things to complete, which in his words would take only a couple of hours. Out there, however, a couple of hours meant half a day, and that's exactly what it took. We fired up the generator unit, power was generated, we made a couple of tweaks here and there, and everything was working fine. The unit was brought up to full load, and the job was done.

The next day, while I was signing documentation, the superintendent called me into his office and thanked me for my efforts. This was very pleasing and much appreciated. He then went on to talk for quite a while, and with overwhelming admiration, not about the job but about the country's forthcoming carnival. As the work was completed and we were not in a desperate hurry, we just listened. The way he talked showed that he had deep sense of pride for his carnival.

This he did not have to do, because at this time of the year – especially in the hotel we were staying in – the carnival agenda was in full swing, and every day and night there was something new being promoted. Before we left the office, he asked us if we had seen the carnival before. We said no and added that as it was at the end of the month, there didn't seem to be much chance of our seeing this one unless we came back on holiday. We then left his office.

The carnival season starts at the end of January each year, depending upon when Easter falls. Each night in our hotel, different functions were taking place to enable all the major parts and procedures of the carnival to be sorted out. It started with the bands. Each band played and was graded. This took a week, so each night in the hotel, we experienced a party atmosphere as each band performed.

We thought that was good, but it was nothing, because picking the carnival queen was even noisier and more exciting.

The period of carnival festivities culminates with the *grand march* (main parade) on the last Sunday before Ash Wednesday and the farewell parade on the evening of the Tuesday before Ash Wednesday (the first day of Lent).

We visited the site the next day, hoping that the superintendent was going to sign our release papers, as the machine had been running through the night without any problems. When we arrived at his office to see him, his door was shut. He was on the phone to our manager. He opened the door and waved us in, putting the call on speaker.

My manager was telling us that I was to stay – no ifs, no buts. I was to stay, never mind my contract and the fact that my instructions before leaving home had been "Don't worry; you will be back home in no more than three weeks." My new instructions were to train more technicians on the control system and assist them in calibration of all the unit instrumentation.

This was going to be a very long trip now if the new technicians were as good as the first ones – not to mention that it was getting near the carnival itself, so some days they wouldn't be available. Yet again the main office had landed me in the mire without consulting with the people on site before making promises.

Not only were the technicians not up to scratch, but every morning they were totally knackered. This was, of course, during the lead-up to the carnival, and preparation was in full swing. The picking of the bands, the princess, and the lead group all had to be catered for. And this was going on in my hotel, so not only were the students knackered, but I was as well. I decided to follow the old saying, "When in Rome, do as the Romans do." I was up late every night watching the festivities, and I must admit that the presentation was amazing. I had heard that this carnival was the second best in the world, next to Brazil's, and after watching and taking part in this one, I could not argue.

After the phone call, the superintendent had said to me, "You might see our carnival yet." And he was correct; I saw the carnival.

My big concern was how slow the pace was each day. As the carnival was getting closer, the engineers being trained were getting slower and slower. Each of them was out at night dancing the time away, and when they turned up, they were so tired they just wanted to sleep. This was not helping them understand the system, so I returned to the superintendent and explained the situation. He was very sympathetic, but his actions told me he was not going to do anything, so I had to slow down even further. In fact, I was sleeping so late in the mornings that I told the class no work would commence until lunchtime. This went down as a treat, and everyone was happy.

On the day of the carnival, drinking commenced at eight in the morning and went on all day. All the bands and all the dancers were arranged as per the results of the judges, and it was organised down to the finest detail – impressive, considering everyone was drunk. The parade itself was spectacular. The costumes were out of this world, and the people were so friendly that it was a pleasure staying here for one and half months, even though I was only meant to be there for three or four weeks at the most.

From my point of view, I did not have any say in the matter. When I left for this assignment, it was for a maximum of three weeks, as I said earlier, but management and staff did not give two hoots about individuals' lives. They had no problem keeping employees on a site though they knew that the assignment was only intended to last a short period of time. As long as the client was paying the extra money, that was it.

My main concern was that I was not consulted about staying the extra time and whether my domestic situation allowed me to stay. Also very annoying was that they never even had the decency to phone my wife and explain to her that it was a company decision to keep me on site and explain the situation. At least that way she would have known that the company was at the minimum caring about their employee and family and treating employees with a little bit of respect.

Overall, staying an extra three weeks made a lot of money for the company, yet they did not have the decency to notify my family about the delay. In my eyes, there was no excuse for doing that; it just emphasized that management thought of all travelling workers as cattle fodder.

I must admit that I left Curacao with a heavy heart. I sometimes think that if I were not married and my family settled, this would be the place to rest my weary heart and stay forever.

Chapter 4

ESSO FAWLEY (SOUTHAMPTON)

The Esso oil refinery at Fawley, United Kingdom, is located in Hampshire, England. The refinery is owned by Esso, which acquired the site in 1925. Situated on Southampton Water, it was rebuilt and extended in 1951 and is now the largest oil refinery in the United Kingdom and one of the most complex refineries in Europe.

Esso Fawley has a mile-long marine terminal that handles around two thousand ship movements and 22 million tonnes of crude oil and other products every year. The refinery processes around two hundred seventy thousand barrels of crude oil a day and provides 20 per cent of UK refinery capacity. Our contract at this refinery was to install a frame-size MS6001 50 Hertz generator set capable of producing thirty-five megawatts of power. My remit was to commission the plant and hand it over to ESSO personnel.

These contracts were always good; I could stay in touch with my family, as they were only a quick phone call away. The downside is that the money received was not enough, as there was very little overtime at the beginning, which was quite common because the installation was still being completed. That left us kicking ourselves over the weekend and in the evenings, apart from an occasional visit to see the Southampton football team playing at the Dell and an occasional curry which was not up to the ones back home.

Southampton, in these days, did not have a lot to offer – especially when the financial situation was not good. So, to keep myself from spending, I spent a lot of time jogging around the area.

As usual, the project was behind schedule, and after sitting around for two weekends, we decided to head north on the third weekend. After finishing work at one o'clock, as the site manager was away as of ten o'clock Friday morning, we set out to get north as early as possible. This was fine until we got to Carlyle, when the temperature plummeted and snow began falling. To crown it all, the old Ford CORTINA we were driving started to play up. When we reduced speed, it cut out, so we had to keep it going above forty miles an hour. This was very difficult when every motorist was crawling up the road at thirty miles an hour. So there we were, on the outside lane, battling through the snow at a speed unsuitable for the road conditions. On arriving in Glasgow (how, only God knows) the car finally cut out, and we couldn't get it started, so we abandoned it at the side of the road. I phoned the wife, and she picked me up and eventually got me home. phoned my brother, a mechanic, and he said the car would be picked up in the morning and would be checked out. "Good," I said, "but I have to get it back before six on Sunday."

I arranged to meet him in the morning to hand over the keys so he could start work immediately and asked if I could be of assistance. No was the reply. "Leave it with me," he said.

I received a phone call on Saturday; and it was bad news. There were big problems with the engine, and it needed to be stripped down. It appeared that there was a loss of compression in two of the four cylinders. I explained again how important it was that we get it back to Southampton early on Monday morning, asking him again if there was anything that could be done to get it down there again. He said, "Leave it with me, and I'll phone you back later."

My mate phoned up to see what was happening and informed me that we had to be down south before the manager appeared on Monday morning. Late Saturday evening, I heard good news from my brother. The car was ready to go. I asked what he had done, and he said, "You don't want to know. Pick it up tomorrow, and we'll have a chat."

The next day, when I picked up the car, he informed me that there was no guarantee that it would get me down south. "There are two things that you must try to do," he said. "Don't hammer the car; keep it at a steady sixty miles per hour. The other thing: try to keep it running." So all the way down on Sunday evening, we kept the car running as much as we could, and we got it back to Southampton. The work carried out by my brother worked, and we got back down south in good time. Still, a good idea had been wasted because of a mechanical failure on the car.

Monday morning, the site manager appeared for breakfast. We left the hotel for the car, and a strange thing happened – the car would not start.

As the manager's car was close by, we went to the site in his car. On arrival at the site, he phoned the local garage and arranged with them to pick up the Cortina and put it through its MOT, also explaining that it had a problem starting. He asked them to send him a report. The garage sent the report in by fax, and their conclusion was terminal. The cylinder head was damaged, and the cost was going to be too much, so the motor was scrapped and a new hired one was supplied.

During the next week, the schedule was revamped and overtime was added. This certainly stopped us from travelling north on weekends.

This change ended the construction and installation within a couple of weeks and just left me on site to finish the commissioning phase.

While out jogging, I sustained problems with my knees. This was diagnosed by the site doctor as housemaid's knee – a condition brought about when fluid builds up in the knee, which often occurs when kneeling on hard surfaces (hence the name). Of course, it was horrendous trying to commission a control system when I couldn't kneel. Not only that, but I could not bend my knees, so I had to lie down when checking wiring, which was something else.

Carrying on, I managed to get through with painkillers and hot baths in the evening. This obviously curtailed my jogging for a while, and also my going outside the hotel. Spending a lot of time in the hotel was not too bad, as the staff were very friendly and stayed in most nights. When I asked them why they stayed in the hotel on their nights off instead of going dancing and perhaps meeting a nice boy and living happily ever after, the reply was "It is obvious you haven't been to the dancing in Southampton."

"No," I replied.

"Well, you have a better chance of meeting a nice guy and settling down and living happily ever after than we have; most of the guys going to the dancing are gay." Enough said.

This was a pity, as in the north of the country that was not an issue. Even though it's about in this era, it is certainly not a factor for young ones going to the dancing.

The commissioning went smoothly, and the opening ceremony was arranged. It was very unfortunate that, for some reason, my name was not on the guest list.

It was these little things that sometimes got me pissed off – especially whilst I was checking for slight defects and busloads of invited guest appeared over my shoulder. The least they could have given me was a doggy bag. It must have been quite amusing when my senior manager came into the control cab to do his nosy explaining to Exxon top brass about something they knew very little about and he saw me lying on the floor, measuring things as the machine was running.

The opening ceremony took place, and I managed to get the machine running for a short while so that the dignitaries were happy; but once they were subjected to the noise, they soon left. This was just as well, as there was still work to be done. In fact, there were quite a lot of faults to investigate. Not all the faults were mine; there were some question marks about the fuel being pumped into the machine. Generally the machines could run on any fuel, but if the fuel was really of a poor quality, then the output suffered. customers didn't want to acknowledge this fundamental issue, though it was a fact. They imagined that all the waste from the process could get fed into the machine without any problems.

After finally getting the machine in satisfactory condition, I left site. The next major assignment was another Exxon site, but this one was a lot closer to home.

Chapter 5

TRAINING COURSE (BAHAMAS)

When I arrived back to the office after spending twelve weeks talking and working on old machines, I was informed that I was flying out to New York on Sunday to attend a training course on a new control system, MKV, at GE offices in Schenectady America.

This was quite a surprise, as I had not been informed either by phone or email that I was going on this course working on MKI, MKII and MKII ITS systems up till now. I had no information on MKV and had had no discussions with anyone in the office about MKV, but this was typical. There was no need to get upset, as this was the standard I was used by now.

I tidied up my reports, registered my expenses, and went home the next day. I received a phone call, still with no hint of an apology, telling me to come in to the office on Thursday to pick up tickets and documents.

At the office, I was promptly told to get myself along to the main offices as quick as possible, as there was a meeting convened for all staff attending training on MKV in New York. I went along utterly boiling. This meeting was being held to go over points in the literature received six weeks ago in the office, which I hadn't seen till this very day. Before the meeting started, I explained to the manager of the design department that I hadn't seen the material and asked whether I should be going on this course. He assured me that not a lot of time from any of the departments had been spent on the material.

After the meeting, I attached myself to engineering design personnel, who seemed to know more about the course than anyone else, and they gave me a brief but most valuable insight into the basic concept of the new panel. I went back to my office still mad that the manuals for the course had not been sent to me sooner. I challenged the projects team, but as usual, no one had been put in charge to ensure I received the proper manuals.

I flew out on the Sunday, still mad that once again the information channels were totally inadequate. I was assured by the main design manager that there would be quite a time before we were ready to include the MKV in our power station packages.

As I sat through the course, it was plainly obvious that we were now moving away from our standard analogue systems to a microprocessor-based system.

Being that the new system was totally different, I was hanging on and getting lost most of the time throughout the course and finding certain parts quite a struggle. I was assured again that the class and instructors were all aware that this was the first time I had seen the books and that I would need more time to get to the level of the rest of the class.

Our American hosts were very good. They took time to explain the system with great skill and technical knowledge; this made the course very worthwhile. The way they presented the course by referring to the old system and then relating it to the new system was obviously designed for people like me, who had been brought up with the old system and were still working on it. The instructors were very thorough and explained the system very well.

Just as you can imagine, everything in America had to bigger and better (and most of the time it was). Nowhere better was the hospitality at night. The restaurants our hosts took us to were exceptional. Each one seemed to better than the one before. The one that outdid them all was a steak restaurant quite a little way out of the town centre, where if any members of the group could eat the super steak, everyone's meal would be free. After seeing the size of the steak, no one from our side would tackle it not only that not even one of our hosts tackle it. The steak weighed in at a massive twenty-five ounces and was enormous.

With none of the party trying to eat it, our hosts just paid for the meal. It certainly was up there as the best steak house I had ever been in.

The final day brought a whole lot of relief, as I had managed to survive – even though my head was buzzing.

At least in the end I had a very good hold on what the system was all about. The only thing now was determining how much preparation time I could get to keep abreast of the system.

Knowing the way commissioning was, I assumed the next time I saw a panel would be when the client was breathing down my neck. While feeling very good that I had managed to keep up most of the time, I received a message from the main office.

The news was not good. I had to go directly to the Bahamas for a courtesy visit.

Two weeks in the sun did not seem too bad. Maybe they were feeling guilty back in the office after my previous encounters. This was a little sweetener.

After saying my farewells to the other members of the class and the instructors, I had to leave early to catch a plane from New York to Miami and then a plane to the Bahamas. This I did, but it was not an easy task coming off a domestic flight with all the baggage I had and then getting to the international flight area and then to the Bahamas departure lounge. It was a nightmare. The distance must have been over a mile, and carrying the baggage that I had, it took me over forty-five minutes to get there. Plus the time needed to get off of one plane and onto the other never comes into office thinking. This is further evidence that the office staff don't have time to research the routes they send employees on or that they just don't care. The phrase "Out of sight, out of mind" comes to mind.

The other thing they never told me was that the plane they booked me on to the Bahamas was a holiday charter – obviously the cheapest one the company could get at the time.

So there I was, turned up with suit, collar, tie, and briefcase. The seats booked were the cheapest, and I was last to board the plane. The pilot turned up wearing shorts, a T-shirt, and a baseball hat; everyone had a good laugh at my expense. Again the details were not good enough.

For once, arriving in the Bahamas on Friday gave me the weekend to unwind and go over the notes I had problems with on the course.

As the visit to Freeport, Bahamas, was a courtesy call and the unit was a frame-size MS5001 50 Hertz power generator set, I felt that no preparation work was required. I knew these machines very well. The control system was a Speedtronic MKII – not the very earliest model, but quite old – so I had plenty of experience working on them. At least that's what I was hoping, as I had no idea what I would face on Monday.

Expecting no problems at the power station a few beers and a game of golf were on the agenda. The beers went down a treat, but the game of golf was spoiled with crocodiles wanting to look after my golf balls and, on the side, eat me. The golf course mostly ran along the beach and had a lot of undergrowth where crocodiles liked to hang out.

They did not take too kindly to my looking for my ball near to where they hung out, so losing quite a few and leaving a few lying about was the wise thing to do, making sure my detour away from them was substantial. I was informed later that crocodiles can run quite fast when provoked; obviously, my game didn't provoke them enough that they felt like chasing me and my caddy.

Monday arrived too soon, to be honest. The taxi arrived bang on at the arranged time. fifteen minutes later, I arrived at power station, where I was met by the security staff and taken to the site manager's office. After a couple of minutes, the site manager and foreman appeared.

I had just finished my introduction when the site manager hurled abuse at me and my company. This abuse went on and on, ranging from the state of the machine to personnel and to the office that did not answer his emails. I thought to myself, *That's not new; they don't even answer my emails*, but I thought it would be better kept to myself. His ranting went on and on. By now it was becoming boring, and he was repeating himself. I interrupted him and said, "If you continue, I'm leaving. What you are saying has very little to do with me, as I have never been on site and I don't work in the office." This had no effect on him, and he continued quoting emails and faults with the machine. By this time, I'd had enough. I lifted my case and left the office, went downstairs, and asked the security man to call a taxi. While I was awaiting the taxi, the site foreman approached and apologised for the manager and invited me for a cup of coffee. I accepted his invitation, and we went to his office and a had a chat over a cup.

What came from the chat was frustration at the state of the machine's stability. Erroneous trips ware causing many problems, the generation of power was far short of expected output, and there was frustration that no one at my office was answering calls and faxes. All these items were stacking up. "I'm afraid you have turned up at the wrong time," the foreman said. "Over the weekend, the output of the generator set could not supply the required load. Not only that, but the unit tripped, setting off the fire system and emptying the CO_2 bottles, causing a problem whereby the site has to fill the bottles before we can start the unit again. This was the third trip in as many days, and we had no CO_2 left on site. As the new CO_2 had to come by boat from Nassau at a heavy cost, the plant could not fulfil the committed obligation."

The foreman again apologised and accepted all these points. I had no input into them, but you can imagine the site manager's frustration.

I explained, showing him the fax that I received stating this was a courtesy visit; it made no mention of the problems that were evidently being experienced.

Again I had been put out to dry because the office personnel were frightened to tell their fellow employees the full story about the site visit.

After the chat, I asked him to take me to the machine. It seemed to be in good condition apart for a CO_2 leak inside the control cab, and it appeared that the leak had been there for a while.

The control panel was in good condition, and so was the motor control centre, so this was good. The problems appeared to be related to only fire and gas and calibration.

The whole unit was clean and tidy, so I asked to see the shutdown log taken a few hours prior to assess the situation. I presented the foreman with a plan of action which would take approximately five days, and this was subject to the site manger staying away from the machine and, more importantly, staying away from me.

The foreman took my proposed plan to the head of the department, and it was approved. Work would start early the next day.

The plan contained a full calibration of the control panel, instrumentation, and fire system sensors. All part numbers and scales were to be recorded. Control panel calibration would be carried out by me. All instrument and fire system calibration would be carried out by power station technicians with my supervision. It was explained that because of other duties, we might not get all the men required on Tuesday. But by Thursday we were to have all the men we needed and maybe more.

By the time all the work was carried out, the CO_2 bottles were to have arrived from Nassau and we would be able to run the machine.

Work commenced and went very smoothly. Certain things were highlighted and rectified within schedule. Other certain parts went slower than estimated, and Saturday and Sunday work had to be carried out. This did disturb me, as I had expected to have a round of golf and top up my tan before departing.

Special attention had to be given to the problem highlighted by the client and the very derogative remarks about my company relating to the fire and gas system. Investigation showed that the client had removed the sensors and replaced them incorrectly. The items which should have been fitted in the hottest part of the installation were actually fitted in the coolest part of the machine. Placing the wrong sensors in critical compartments was the reason the CO_2 system was going off when the machine was loading up. This fault took quite a bit of time to identify.

As usual, the CO_2 bottles were delayed from Nassau, and this caused us a day's delay in firing the machine. In my case, a day's sunbathing and a game of golf were on the cards. The whole day off did not materialise, but I did get in a little bit of sunbathing and a second game of golf. And yes, the biggest hazard was crocodiles on the golf course yet again. It was fortunate that I was only allowed on the course with a caddie; he knew exactly where not to go, and I managed to survive.

The next morning, the CO_2 bottles arrived. I fired the unit to maximum power. The unit did not trip, the control system was stable, and all functional tests were carried out successfully. The engineering foreman was over the moon at the start of the contract. I was told the whole story, but in the end it was clear that his job was on the line if this did not work out correctly.

To his credit, the site manager apologised for his behaviour and admitted he was right out of order, as he knew that I had never been at his site before and that to blame me for all the faults of others was not correct. He didn't have to say any more; the fact that he made the effort to apologise was good enough. I bore in mind that I felt the very same about the way some field engineers were treated by the head office.

We agreed that the unit would run overnight and that if everything was satisfactory in the morning, I could leave ASAP. I sat the rest of day, compiling my report. Once it was signed and accepted by the site manager and my time sheet was compiled and signed, it was time for me to go home. It was just a pity I never got the time to see the whole of the island.

This time I wore no collar and tie, and certainly no suit. What was good enough for the pilot was good enough for me – shorts to the ready.

At least I did not face the journey from the domestic to the international terminal as I was leaving from the same terminal. The journey between the main holiday charter terminal and the international departure area was far enough. With all the stuff I was carrying, a pack mule would have had problems.

I again logged a report at the office. Again no meeting was arranged to discuss problems on site and customer concerns. It was time to move on to the next job.

001 (3)

001 (4)

Alcatraz By Sea

At the Pier in San Francisco

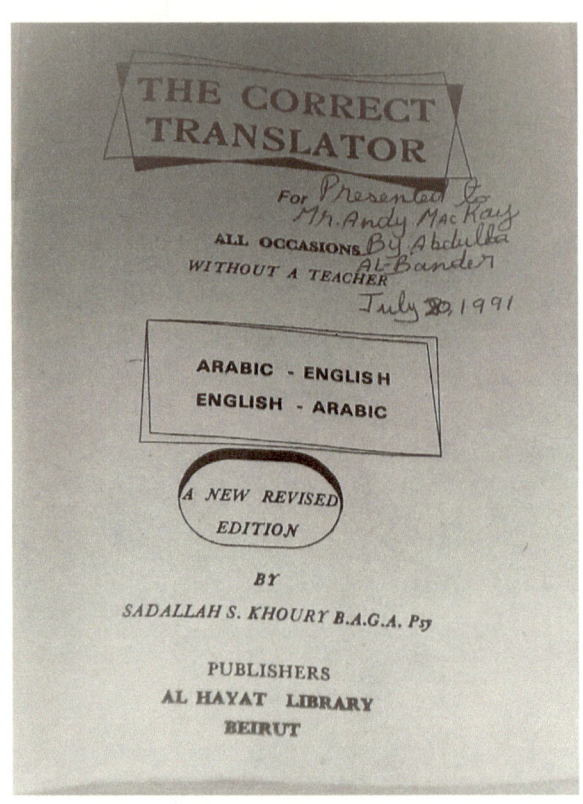

Book Presented from class student

Bowling Class

Certificate for Walking the Great Wall

Chanel Island Plant Layout

Channel Island Planr without me

Chinnese Banquet to show appreciation

Chinnese Class Size Loa He

Chinnese class Size

Chinnese Engineers Take me to Thousand Peaks Moutain Range

Crossing Palembang Bridge

Driving to Lake Tahoe

Entertainers in The Pier Area

Ferry Crossing Palembang

Fun Time at SanFrancisco Pier area

Golden Gate Bridge

Hotel stayed before departing for Shingli and Zong Yuon

Lake Tahoe view

Lake Tahoe

Looking out from the Pier to Alcatraz

Main Gate to Channel Island Power Station

New Chinnese Power Station Under Construction

Notra Dame Cathedral Vietnam

Palembang Barge

Reno Gambling City

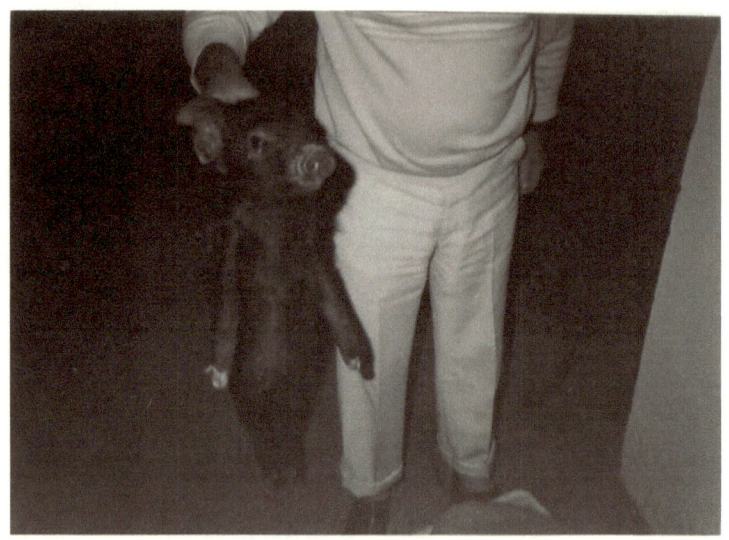

Suckling Pig the one that got away

Tainanman Square Isolation

Tainanman Square showing the people being diverted across the road and away from the square

Tainanmin Square After the Students Demonstrations

Tainanmin Square Today

Tairnanmin Square Heavy Presence of the Militery

Tram Ride plaqued with danger

Tram Travel In Sanfrancisco

Typical Chinnese Market

Vietnam Independance Palace

Vietnam Museum Exibit

Vietnam War Museam

Vietnamese travelling to Work

View of Lake Tahoe ski Resorts

View of Tainanmin Square from Kate Aides Room
BBC Coverage of the stedents Demonstration

View of the Forbidden City One of the few
Westerners allowed in Tiananmin Square

Visit to Reno

Wild Australian Friend

Zong Youn Class

Chapter 6

MOSSMORRAN (FIFE)

This was a pleasant surprise – a contract right on my doorstep. I could travel to and from the house each day. And it should have been a dawdle, apart from one thing – the gas turbine with a compressor drive, MS5002. The two at the end of 5002 indicates a two-shaft machine It was supplied to Lummus/Esso Chemical Ltd and was installed at Mossmorran with the latest MKV control system – the same one that I went on the training course to learn about, and the same one that I hadn't seen the course agenda for until a few days before the course started. It had been over six months since I'd seen anything about the system. As I'd been working on other contracts which had absolutely nothing whatsoever to do with MKV, you can imagine my shock when I learned that my company had had the audacity to sell me to the client as an expert. My only saving grace was that the contract was behind schedule and commissioning was further behind, so this would give me some time to catch up on the notes and literature supplied from the course.

Exxon Mobil Chemical's Fife Ethylene Plant (FEP) was, at the time of installation, the largest European plant being built. Also it had the most modern state-of-the-art equipment fitted. It was the first time our MKV control equipment had ever been installed in an actual site. If it did not perform as sold, then from a company point of view this meant big trouble, as this plant was meant to run for a whole year without a shutdown – not too much to ask for.

On arriving on site, I reported to the main office, where I was introduced to the company's engineers. These were Exxon men that would be working alongside me on the turbine train, finding out that there control specialists were on the same training course that I was on a couple of weeks after me you could imagine my shock not only that they have been analysing the data from the course for weeks who was the expert.

After the usual safety introductions and instructions, which were numerous, I was shown round the site. Owing to the radius of the feed pipe running into the compressor, the machine had to be located about twenty feet from ground level. The whole site was very impressive, and the amount of men working was also impressive. One thing was certain: if I was not fit at this moment in time, I certainly would be when I left the site.

During my tour of the site, I met my company's mechanical engineer, who was employed as a technical assistant to the main contractor at this time. He had very little contact with Exxon. His involvement was to ensure all the bits sent from our company were assembled correctly and located in the correct places.

After all the meetings with the client representatives had been completed, I arranged a meeting with my fellow colleague so that he could give me our company's take on what was required from our point view, as we knew that clients want heaven and earth but don't want to pay for it.

He explained that his remit was different from mine, as he was here just to supervise the mechanical installation, whereas I was to calibrate the control panel, get it up and running, and assist the Exxon engineers to understand the workings of the system (a lot of work).

After all the technical jargon had been gone over and I had listened to his interpretation of the contract, I was on my own, effectively working purely for Exxon personnel. He was working for the main contractor. I said to him, "That is fine, but there must come a time when you transfer from the main contractor to Exxon to complete the commissioning, as normal practice dictates." I didn't get much of a response from my colleague on this matter, so rather dwell on this subject, I moved on, knowing that the main office was only a couple of hours away and that they could sort out our technical obligations. If I needed help, I could get it from them.

He then he informed me that he was having problems domestically and would be taking time off. Showing concern, I inquired, "How much time will you require?" He said he was not sure but indicated it might be one or two days a week for the next six to seven weeks so that he could deal with lawyers as he was going through a marriage separation.

At this time in the project, this absence schedule did not pose much of a problem, as the project was well behind, so I just carried on doing what was required with a new project, getting all the latest drawings matching with the client's requirements.

As the time to start the machine was getting nearer, the electrical workload was getting heavier and heavier. Then came the shocker, the client's mechanical engineer asked me when I was going to check the mechanical piping schematics. I retorted by saying that he should speak with my mechanical engineer. He replied that the engineer had not been seen for a couple of days because of domestic problems.

The domestic problems had lasted for three months. He did not affect what I was doing; I just wasn't in contact with him every day. I informed the client's engineer to look at all the drawings issued and said I'd have a look at them in the afternoon. Not wanting to land my colleague in the stew, I tried to cover up the fact he was missing as best I could. He did not appear till the middle of the following week. After covering up the mechanical stuff plus checking a latest revision of the software, I was about at my breaking point when he appeared.

I explaining the situation to him and advised him of my thoughts. "I think you should get someone else from head office, as the workload is getting very tight."

He did not reply but just walked away.

The next day, I got a message from Exxon that a meeting was being arranged and I had to attend. This I did, and to my surprise, work which should have been carried out according to the site reports obviously hadn't been. Before leaving the meeting, I said that I would have to travel to my head office, present the client's concerns to my manager, and have a meeting with all the main parties to see the way forward. They then asked to see the minutes of the meeting to see if they had to do anything on their end.

I travelled the next morning to the head office for the meeting. As usual, nothing was arranged, even though I had informed them the day before.

My manager was called to another meeting, so the secretary said, leaving me biting my nails. He eventually turned up and produced documents and it was apparent something I never knew about was that the work asked for by the client my colleague had already put in his report saying that the work had already been done. This was putting me under severe pressure. What was I to say? My manager was telling me that the job was on schedule, yet the client had informed me it was not. I was being put in a terrible position. Eventually I said it was time that he visited the site and talked to the client and found out what was happening, as I personally had too much work to get through before firing up the machine. I needed a hand. My manager insisted that my colleague would be transferring from the main contractor to Exxon soon, and that would be my extra help.

"That's not going to satisfy Exxon," I said. "You have to sit down and talk to them. Identify the mechanical workload and a time scale."

Out came the usual response about why the two of us couldn't do this. I explained the magnitude of what I was doing regarding working on the new system with very little training. Still he didn't want to attend a meeting.

The meeting ended with him saying he would phone my mechanical colleague and arrange things, leaving his office to go back to the site knowing full well that yet again management had sidestepped the issue and people on site had to pick up the pieces. Not only could they not get us to the site correctly, but when we were on site, they left us to get on with it without backup.

Before travelling back to the site, I went up to the design office and talked to the design engineers. They were very helpful and arranged a site visit to assure the client that there were a backup in place for assistance if required and that someone would travel to visit within the next couple of days.

Why my manager could not have talked to the design team and arranged this I don't know.

Travelling back to the site feeling a little easier about my response to the client's concerns from the head office, I tried to contact my colleague to give him the feedback but was without success, as he was not at work that day. This was now a major problem, and when he returned, he was in the process of being removed from the site.

Two days later, he returned to the site carrying a site report update of what had to be done moving forward, and he presented it to Exxon. At this point, I took a back seat and allowed the site manager to read the report and attack the contents, and this he did. The lack of mechanical involvement and progress was the main subject. My colleague put up a fine defence, saying that he was involved with the installation and all the points raised were relating to commissioning, which was not in his agenda. The time spent on site was brought up, and he retorted by saying that that was not Exxon business. If they required extra men for commissioning, then they should have gone to the head office and requested more people. They then looked at me and said, "Did you request more men?" As the report showed, all the work needing done had been done. In my eyes, it was just later that it was discovered that it had not been done, and that is why we were now addressing the problem. So instead of my colleague being on the verge of being thrown off site, he had turned it around, and the finger was being pointed at me for not requesting assistance, and I was not requesting assistance so I could cover up for his time away from the site. The meeting was closed with the statement that the head office design team would have closer involvement in the site progress.

The assistance of the design team left me with some free time, and my colleague was forced to be on site every day, now employed with Exxon. The commission was soon completed.

Soon after all the mechanical parts were fitted/running my colleague left the site. I was kept on for standby duties. This lasted for an extra three months, leaving me time on site to clear up all defects, updating drawings with the machine working well. This was an achievement. I expected to leave the site at the end of the month till a meeting with the site manager at which they asked for me to extend my standby. Mossmorran engineers had an agreement with my company that I could be seconded on standby for a further six months. Again this was arranged without any input by me, and this was done behind my back by a manager who wouldn't come to a meeting and explain his position to Exxon. this really got my back up.

The deal was that I was to stay on site to assist Exxon on the running of the control system and any other mechanical problems after initial handover. To be honest, this time it was just perfect. I was guaranteed a certain amount of overtime, I was home every night, and it was nice to get a bit of quality home time.

Three weeks in our first shutdown/trip happened as a result of mechanical problems, and oh, what a fright this was. As the unit shut down, it also closed down the whole process, and the whole plant shut down. All the gas that was on the process site went to the flare system, and the size of the flare was so large that the local people phoned the fire brigade, as they thought the whole plant was on fire.

When the firefighters appeared at the site, all of them jumped out of the cabs wearing full battle dress. There was not one but four of them – quite a site. After checking the installation, they left, and we fired up the unit again. This mishap closed down the whole site. This presented a major deviation from the philosophy of the site, which was designed so no single fault would cause this sort of failure.

As all the equipment on site had a system of voting that required two out of three faults before tripping occurred, this single fault should not have tripped any critical equipment. It seemed very strange that the only budget was for one gas compressor train; when that tripped, the whole site was shut down.

After three months, it was turning into a complete drag not being involved with the meetings but just checking running data every morning and afternoon, praying for a fault to appear or, on a good day, a shutdown. But this was wishful thinking, and 99 per cent of the time, nothing happened. Data was logged. Visits to the control panel in the afternoon generally were fruitless, as to do any work I had to go and get a permit; and as the machine was running, this was generally refused.

As time was going by, other contracts abroad were being touted when I visited the company offices every two weeks.

As I said earlier, the only good thing was that I was at home and spending a bit of quality time at home and was frightened to complain too much, as the family would not have been too pleased, so I bit the bullet and put up with the boredom for my family.

After six months and two days, I finally said goodbye to Mossmorran. It certainly was one of the better jobs, even after all the hassle at the start – not from Exxon but from my own colleague and his marital problems.

The Mossmorran experience was invaluable, as the new system was very tricky and the extra time spent on site checking drawings and installation was perfect. All the time I was there, the Exxon personnel were exemplary and very thoughtful; they gave me all the respect they could, and this aspect of the contract was first-class.

It was a pity that even a major contract on our doorstep could not have been managed more professionally from the head office. It took many phone calls and meetings to come up with a solution to a domestic problem from an employee who was having big problems, and even though the management at the head office knew about it, they kept their heads in the sand and allowed it to fester, to the detriment of our company name with the end user.

On leaving the site, I was taken to nice restaurant by the senior instrument manager, who showed his appreciation, which was very nice.

The next contract was in California, the Golden State. This sounded wonderful, and I was looking forward to going to the capital, Sacramento, to enjoy a bit of sunshine.

Chapter 7

SACRAMENTO (UNITED STATES)

Our contract was to install a Frame-Size 7001 60 hertz generator set for Sacramento Municipal Utility District. The power station was located in Sacramento's McClellan Air Force Base. This base was to service all the latest aircraft's that the American forces had at that time. The power station was located within the base but isolated from the operation of the base, which was just brilliant, as the security was very tight for us to get into the power station, and I could only imagine what the security was like going into the base itself.

I thought to myself, *What could possibly go wrong in California?* No matter what book I read on the state, it said the state had everything, so I assumed my stay here would be wonderful. I thought to myself, *I've landed on my feet here.*

Having a week to prepare was also a first. I generally got two days and was on a plane, so it was nice to get treated like a human being. I packed my bags, said cheerio to the family, and flew to New York for a forwarding flight to Sacramento. I was picked up at the airport by the client, who booked out a hire car in my name and drove me to the accommodation. Leaving the car for me, he said, "The rest of your installation team will see you tonight. Have some rest, and I'll see you in the morning at the security check area." Very civilised.

I unpacked my belongings and lay down on top of the bed. The next thing I knew, my fellow colleagues were knocking at the door, shouting, "Come on; it's tea time."

I had slept for five hours; it was a long flight – especially in economy class. I got up quickly and showered, and I met my fellow colleagues. Lo and behold, my friend from Mossmorran was here. Luckily for me, he had only another month more to stay and then was off.

The job was identical to the Mossmorran job. I was seconded to the client, and the installation group was assigned to the main contractor, supervised by the client, which was fine. Driving to the site the next morning was very tricky.

Driving on the wrong side of the road in a car with an automatic transmission using one foot was awkward. When I arrived at the base, the rest of my colleagues entered using their passes I had to go through a two-hour introductory course before being given my pass. This was not a problem; better safe than sorry.

After the course, I was introduced to the client's project team, and the one of the first statements made was about how my colleague is handling being away from family when going through the separation from his wife. I thought to myself, "Surely he isn't playing this same old tune out here." I was desperate to tell them that he had been going through this separation for a year now and that they shouldn't listen to him bleating on. If he had been concerned, he would have been back home doing an office job till it was all sorted out. But no, like a fool, I just said, "I know all about it. It's a pity. It must be a very hard time for him."

The only good thing about this trip was that my colleague could not take days off to see a solicitor, so he got on with the work. One of the major troubles on this site was the proximity of the power station to the testing area for the F111 aircraft. The noise generated when they were being tested was ear shattering, and every day, maybe twice a day, this testing went on. The only escape was to retreat to the power station acoustic enclosure, but at the early commissioning of the plant, there were only certain functions that could be carried out, so finding oneself outside when the testing of the jets was going on was quite common.

One of the major pluses on this contract was the accommodation. Each one of us had a flat to ourselves, which was good. There is nothing better than just sometimes closing the door and having some quality time alone.

Now, the major downside to this contract was the lack of overtime. Overtime in these parts was non-existent. The culture here such that only under special circumstances would there be a requirement to work late, so the local workers were not willing to work a lot of overtime – maybe an hour or so, depending on what was happening. This is never a good situation – especially for people like me and others who need the overtime allowances to justify being away from home.

With very little overtime, we obviously had far too much free time away from the power station. The complete installation was not in too much of a hurry, owing to contractual talks over the power distribution supply breaking down every time our client met the end user. Whether this was factual or an excuse, we will never know, as we were not invited to the meetings.

This was bad, as it appeared that I and the team would be spending Christmas 1985 in California. And going along with the standing working practices, we would have quite a few days off throughout that period.

Good news came through when my wife, Violet, phoned to tell me I was going to be a dad for the second time; that weekend was a time for celebration.

We carried on with the commission again, changing drawings to represent what they wanted and not what we thought they wanted This was the same in most contracts, so nothing had changed. This was not only our fault; the client on most occasions had given over the wrong details to our design team, and only when we got to the site did it become clearer what was required. Most of the time the requirements were small things like interfacing with other plant equipment, which was essential to the operation of the plant but not to the gas turbine. This just meant more work for me, which, to be honest, was a pain in the neck, as I had too much to commission in the first place.

Being in California at this time of the year, during Thanksgiving and Christmas time, there was always something happening. One weekend, we travelled to San Francisco, and it was cold and damp. In fact, according to the locals, at this time of the year it could be cold and damp for months. But it was a wonderful-looking city with plenty to do. One of the main events was to hitch a ride from the dock area to the business centre. This was fun until I was standing on the tram, having a ball, and I nearly fell off as we were fooling around. I turned my head to look directly through the window, and there were two men kissing. Goodness gracious, here was a man brought up in the countryside, witnessing two men kissing in public for the first time. What a shock to the system – so much so that at the first possibility, I jumped off the tram. My colleagues joined me, saying, "I thought we were going down town." I told them what I had seen, and they just about wet themselves.

"Surely you have seen the news about flower power and the gay capital newsreels about San Francisco?" one of them said.

I retorted, "But in daylight in a tourist stronghold?"

They all broke out in laughter again, so it was time to drop the subject.

The next weekend, we went to Reno/Lake Tahoe. It had been snowing, and when travelling over the mountains, it was mandatory that snow chains be fitted to the tyres. That was the only way we could drive in the snow. At the side of the road, there were plenty of mechanics willing and able to put the chains on for you at a cost because it was worthwhile. There was only a slight scattering of snow. As we went over the mountain into Lake Tahoe, what greeted us was one of the most beautiful sights imaginable. This was, of course, the place where the Winter Olympics had been held. There may have only been a scattering of snow on the road and in the town, but at the main ski resort up in the mountains, they had plenty of snow, and the skiers were making the most of it.

Seeing the place for the first time, I was impressed with the magnificent views; yet a lot of Americans come to the city to gamble, and it is obvious why. I have never been to Las Vegas, but I can't imagine or believe they have sights that match Lake Tahoe. They also had gambling – plenty of casinos to lose money at. Not that we had a lot to lose; allowances didn't allow for that sort of entertainment. Still, we had a bite to eat and a little flutter in the casino, and as we wandered around, spending all day just enjoying the ambiance of the place with the sun shining, we could not ask for anything more; it was wonderful.

Just when we thought this place was heaven, the sun disappeared very quickly and the air began to get a bit chilly. The signs all-round the place were telling us that if we wanted to leave today, we had to leave now, as the weather was closing in and heavy snow was forecast (this was normal for this time of the year).

We left as advised, and the traffic was very heavy. As predicted, the snow started to fall very quickly, bringing the traffic to a crawl. The fact that we all had snow chains on kept the traffic moving; without them there was no way any of us could have got over the mountain. After a wonderful day, we were a sorry bunch of travellers leaving a beautiful place.

The following weekend, we travelled down the coast to Monterey. There was beautiful sunshine. We surfed and lazed around like tourists do when they visit the beach. We checked out the celebrities, wanting to meet Clint Eastwood. Unfortunately, we never saw anyone of note.

Being a golfer, I had to visit Pebble Beach Golf Links. This course is like the Old Course at Saint Andrews in Scotland regarding its notoriety. The drive up to the course was just outstanding; I pinched myself now and again, still not believing I was here. I was met by a security guard and asked what was my business was here. I explained where I was from and told him I had seen the course on TV and thought I would come along and see it for myself. He told me where to park and took me to the first tee and the eighteenth green, and it was every bit as beautiful as the TV pictures had shown. After thanking my security guard for his assistance, I drove away, thinking to myself it would be super to play the course. But again, the overseas allowance wouldn't cater for that sort of expense.

As you can imagine, things were very good. But then I received a phone call from the wife telling me that with no overtime and the extravagance of weekends away, spending our own money, the bank statement was very poor. It was obvious that the allowances were not enough and I was dipping into our funds. It was time to clip the wings.

Just shortly after that, the client negotiated his power distribution, and the plant was then a matter of priority. Overtime was essential to adhere to the new schedule; this was to satisfy the power company.

Christmas was upon us, and we had two days off. Americans don't have the same amount of holidays that we have in the United Kingdom, where most places shut down for eight to ten days. Christmas Day, Boxing Day, and New Year's Day were it. This suited us fine, as all the days off earlier had taken their toll.

Management told us that we had to produce power on 2 January. This was a must according to the new schedule, and that was bad news, as we had been invited to the client's New Year's party on the first, and all drink was free. With that sort of invitation to a Scotsman working away from home, there was no way any of us were staying sober – and that's the way it turned out.

We had just over two weeks – fourteen days, excluding holidays – of hard graft to get the power plant up to a state where we would be able to, with a few minor checks, start it up and produce power.

Working for this length of time practically round the clock was not fun, but we managed to achieve our goal and left the site on 31 December knowing that when we came back to work on 2 January, we just had to press the button and power would be generated. The client agreed that as long as we came in on the afternoon and produced power, he would have completed his contractual obligation. If we were not too well, we could go back to our flats and come in on the third bright-eyed and ready to go again.

We left the site on Hogmanay, went back to our flats, got changed, and brought in the bells with just a few drinks, and that was that.

Just before I went to sleep, the phone rang. It was a call from my wife to give me an update and wish me a Happy New Year, knowing that I would just be going to bed and they were just getting ready to celebrate Hogmanay. She put my three-year-old son Andrew on, and he started singing the Steve Wonder song "I Just Called to Say I Love You." You have no idea the emotional feeling of being away from your family and having your son sing these words to you. The tears were choking me. This was one of the nicest things that could possibly happen. It took a good length of time for me to get in control of my feelings again. At this time I wished I could wrap it up and get the next flight home. I did not get a good night's sleep, as I lay awake most of the night. Thinking of home and what I was missing tore a huge lump out of the situation.

Well, 1st off January came. I made a point to phone home, as I knew all the family would have been fed and sitting down to watch TV – and that was the case. I wished everyone a happy New Year and told them I would see them as soon as possible.

I met up with my colleagues and had a few drinks. In the evening, we called taxis to pick us up to go to the party. Just as the invitation had said, drinks were free. And just as we imagined, we were all in full voice, drunk – some more than others. Taxis took us home. We piled out of the cabs and into our flats, a good night having been had by all.

Late the next morning, I went round to get everyone ready. One of the team did not appear. We went to his flat, and the door was lying open, the lock smashed. His jacket was lying over the banister, so we picked up his jacket and entered his room, not knowing what we would find there. He was still in bed. We woke him up, and he still seemed unsure when we asked him what had happened. His recollection was that he had lost his keys so had kicked in the door. We showed him his jacket and said, "Look, the keys were in its pocket." He was unable to comprehend, so we told him to go back to bed, telling him we would notify the caretaker and ask him to repair the door as soon as possible. This was done, and the caretaker said he would work on it right away. After informing my colleague of the situation, we left him behind. We set off to the site and arrived at one o'clock.

As we had done all the checks on the system, it didn't take us long to circulate the oil, prime the fuel system, and get ready for firing.

We started the main motor, got the machine up to cranking, and gave a firing command, watching the fuel system. Vibrating very slightly, the machine accelerated as expected; but just as we got up to critical speed, the control console started to vibrate excessively. As the machine vibration was normal, I allowed the machine to carry on running up. After we got by the critical speed, around 1800 RPM, the vibration in the control cab was getting greater, and I decided to press the emergency shutdown button. The machine came to rest, but the vibrations seemed to take longer to subside. As I exited the control cab, all the staff on duty and my own colleagues were all rolling around laughing. One of them said, "Why did you shut down the machine?" and then burst out laughing, pointing over my shoulder. I looked round, and there were two jets at the bottom of the runway. The flaps were up on the runway; they were testing the engines. As the testing was taking place only seventy-five yards away from the control onsole, that's why we experienced high vibrations.

After the initial shock, I joined in on the joke. Whether it was planned or not, no one admitted to it; and at the end of the day, the machine performed well through the critical starting procedure, so we were all reasonably happy.

Later the jets left and we went for start-up number two. This was successful, and we managed to produce 20 megawatts. This ran for thirty minutes while we took data and then shut the machine down.

After securing the cranking position, we all called it quits and left the site. I checked up on my colleague who did not turn out and found that the door had been fixed and the bill was in the post. I then made my way to my accommodation, glad that everything looked good. I went to bed and slept to the next morning for a solid twelve hours. Awakening brighteyed, we all gathered, had breakfast, and set out for work.

During the next three weeks, all my colleagues left, leaving me to tie up all the loose ends. I did so, and I left the site two weeks after that. I arrived back and logged a report complaining about my colleague's articipation due to his marital problem, stating that he should be exempt from site work till it was all sorted out. But as usual, there was a promise it would be taken care of, and I knew nothing would be done.

While relaxing at home and enjoying my home leave, thinking that California was a thing of the past, I got a telephone call to come into the office for a meeting about – you guessed it – California. The outcome was that I was to return to the site, put in new software, and stand by for three months. During that period, I was to assist in the commissioning of the fire and gas protection system.

I flew back to California and was pleasantly surprised when I went to pick up my rental car and was presented with a massive Cadillac. This was a beautiful motor. I checked the paperwork, and everything was in order, so I drove away thinking that I was important.

The next surprise was that I did not have condominium accommodation this time; I was checked in to the Red Lion Hotel. This was really upmarket; it was an obvious mistake by the office. No way should I have been given a Cadillac to drive about in and put up in a four-star hotel. That was my setup for my three-month stay – based on my domestic situation, as my wife was pregnant. If there were any complications, I would be home as soon as a plane was available; this was agreed upon before leaving the base.

Everything went fine. The client was happy, the project manager came out to sign the official completion certificate, and finally my time was up. My departure date was agreed, and that was that.

Trials and Tribulations of a Travelling Prostitute

The project manager did say that he was surprised at the car I was driving and that I had spent my whole trip in the four-star hotel. But I said that was just the way it was.

Well, as usual, a couple of days before leaving, a problem occurred. One of the control cards for the fire and gas system failed, and I had to go to Silicon Valley, San Francisco, to get a new one. This I did, setting off in the morning bright-eyed and bushy-tailed, feeling on top of the world in knowing I was going home soon. While driving down the road, abiding by the speed limits in a car that could go three times faster, I was getting a little bored.

Halfway into the journey, on a beautiful sunny day, still bored by driving within the speed limit, I saw in my rear-view mirror a car approaching. It was a Porsche, and it was not going at the speed limit, as it zoomed by me. This was what I had been waiting for. My way of thinking was that I would do the same speed as the Porsche, keeping it in view, and if there was a traffic policeman ahead, it would be stopped first, and when I saw its brake lights go on, then I would be able to slow down. And this I did, travelling at one hundred miles per hour. I was sure that my visiting time to Silicon Valley was being halved.

While travelling along, not bored any more, thinking of home, from out of the blue, my whole back window lit up, and I hit the brakes. A sheriff's car pulled alongside. The sheriff held up one finger and then shot away. At first I didn't know what to do. Looking for an exit from the motorway was in vain, so I carried on at fifty miles an hour. Then I turned a corner, and there was the sheriff's car with all the lights blazing and the Porsche just ahead.

The sheriff walked calmly out to the centre of the road and instructed me by pointing to pull over to the side of the road. The sheriff walked over, pointing to the window. I opened the window, and he asked for identification. As I handed him my passport, he asked what speed I had been doing. I told him eighty miles an hour and he said, "Try again." I told him the truth. As he looked at my passport, he said, "Not another foreigner." He then strolled up to his car, slid into it, and about five minutes later appeared again. Approaching my car's window, he asked where was I going and what I was doing in California. I explained that I was ready to go home in a couple of days and I had to collect a new part for the power plant in Sacramento. He then said, "Well, there is no chance of sending you out a summons, as you would be back in the United Kingdom by that time." My heart missed a beat, as if I couldn't be sent a summons, then I would have to go to court today, and only if the courts could fit me in. If not, I would have to stay in jail till the next morning. After the sheriff explained this to me, he walked away down to the Porsche driver.

I just sat there thinking, *I'm going to miss my flight*, worrying about all the hassle of having to book extra nights in the hotel. My brain was scrambled. I wanted to cry. Where the police car had come from, I did not know. And now I'd been caught and was thinking about spending a night in jail. And just when I thought I was going to break down, the sheriff returned with my passport in hand. He stood, raising his hand and throwing my passport onto my lap. "I'm letting you off this time," he said. "Don't you ever speed in my patch again?" The first thing that came to my mind was John Wayne. The sheriff sounded like him, with a deep, powerful voice – one that held my attention one hundred per cent when he was speaking. He then waved me out onto the motorway, and I was glad that the car was an automatic, as I was still shaking. I don't think I could have changed gear if it had been a manual. As for the rest of the journey, I did not exceed the speed limit by even one mile per hour.

I arrived back at the power station around four o'clock, fitted a part, carried out a few panel checks, and left the unit to run overnight. I informed the operators what I had done and that I would carry out a final check first thing in the morning.

The next day, everything was running fine. I was thanked by the power station staff and left the site to do a bit of shopping. All flights home were good and on time, and that was the end of the California experience – one that I will never forget.

Chapter 8

UGHELLI (NIGERIA)

Looking back on my previous experience, I was actually dreading this visit (more so than all the others), the assignment was to fly to Lagos, where I would be met at the airport by the contractor's representative.

He would take me to a hotel and in the morning would escort me to Ughelli Power Station, I would be put up in secure accommodation. This would be supplied with and protected by armed security guards patrolling the accommodation grounds twenty-four hours a day, with this in mind, I specifically asked the manager whether this was a safe place to go to. He assured me that a delegation which had included senior managers had already travelled to Nigeria, visited the site, and reported back that there were no problems. How wrong was this statement, this was the company's line of events and was not factual. The delegation never reached the site, as there was a people's demonstration in Benin halfway to the site and they turned back and stayed in Lagos for the rest of the allocated time. This was not communicated back to me otherwise I would not have not gone on this assignment. This visit was meant to be for six weeks.

I had voiced my concerns about the journey and the place I was going to, and after reading management's report, I still had concerns, knowing now that the area must be dangerous because security guards were patrolling the accommodation with guns. The visit was reduced to twenty three straight days with no weekends off.

This changed during my stay, but the length of time on site did not, I was still concerned and a meeting was arranged the following day (The time was to be set later) this was between our own manager and senior management, who were part of the delegation that had visited the site. I was notified by phone that the meeting would take place at 1300 hours.

I made sure I got there promptly, expecting the same from the other parties. How wrong could I be, before starting, there was me, my colleague, my manager, and one senior manager who hadn't even been one of the delegation, Excuses were given for the members of the delegation.

The senior manager admitted that it was not the best idea to go ahead with the meeting, but as we were meant to leave for Nigeria within the next week, it had to go ahead. He hoped to clarify the company's position. He read a statement from the members of the delegation that had supposedly gone to the site, saying that their report was factual and they had nothing more to add. Opening the meeting, the senior manager, whose remit was to explain that our work was vitally important, stated that the company could win millions of pounds of new contracts in Nigeria, and it all hinged on this visit, which must go ahead and be successful. A compromise was arranged. The time spent would be split between two lecturers. My colleague would go out first and stay for half of the allocated time. Then I would go out and complete the training. Still complaining, he explained that our CVs had been sent to the client. Because of our record and expertise, our names had been accepted by the Nigerian authority, and visas had followed the acceptance letter. If we did not go, the contract would have to be put on hold till the client accepted other CVs, and this would put the company in a compromised position, so I had to go. This put me under severe pressure to go, and I accepted. Before finally agreeing, my list of information and details of my travel arrangements (hotels, currency, etc.) was handed over, to be completed before departure; this was accepted and would be handled immediately. Before I was to visit, another instructor went out before me for the same period of time. After he finished his stay, I would relieve him. He would travel home, and I would be taken to the site. As the schedule was very tight, we never met in the transition. According to his report, everything regarding his visit went as planned, with no problems.

Flights and all details were confirmed. The client responded with final instructions, and off I went. For once everything went very well. Leaving Glasgow, the flight was on time. There were no surprises at the airport before boarding, and I settled down on board the aircraft for a pleasant journey. I left Glasgow Airport on the red-eye Friday morning, bound for

Heathrow Airport and the British Airways flight to Lagos, unaware of the trials and tribulations which lay ahead. The actual flight to Nigeria was fine; I had not a care in the world. The food was good, the service very good, and the plane not too busy. No one was sitting beside me. I watched film and slept most of the way. It was excellent. I arrived at Lagos bright-eyed and feeling quite refreshed, which was unusual. I generally felt washed out and ready for bed after flying for over eight hours. Before picking up my luggage, I spotted a well-dressed man standing with a white board bearing my name and my company's name. As it was inside the actual transit area, I made myself known to him. He greeted me warmly. He explained that he was representing the client and would escort me to the hotel and welcome me to Nigeria. He then escorted me to the baggage area. Looking around the baggage area, I saw that the customs gates were only about twenty metres away from the carousel, which was good. My new friend asked me for my passport and then asked me to put a couple of pounds in the passport at the visa page. Being wary of the situation of handing over my passport (never mind asking a Scotsman to part with money to a stranger), he explained that Nigeria was corrupt and so were their customs workers. "If you don't give them a little gratuity, they will ask you to open your baggage, ask for everything to be emptied out, and then let you go," he said. "So to avoid this, if you do as I say, I will take your passport over to the diplomatic desk on the left, get it stamped, and we will leave with no problems. You can watch from here, and I will not leave your sight." This seemed fair enough, so I put three pounds in the passport, handed it over, and he walked to the diplomatic customs officer. I did not take my eyes off the gent. He approached the customs officer, who on looking at my passport looked over at me, acknowledged me, stamped my passport, and then turned away. My new acquaintance, true to his word, returned with my passport stamped and the money gone (which was not a big deal, as I had had to give gratuities to other customs officers before entering their countries). With my passport safely back in my possession, I relaxed and picked my case from the carousel, and we headed out through the diplomatic door with no inspection and no luggage checks – brilliant. Outside, among the many hundreds of Nigerians, my guide asked me if I wished to change any British pounds into Nigerian naira for tipping purposes only. He informed me that the exchange rate at the airport was the best in the country and that it was the safest place to change currency. One of the instructions on my invitation to Nigeria was that I should take only two hundred pounds with me, as Nigerian currency was not strong. He was verifying exactly what had been discussed in the office, and I was becoming more relaxed with my chaperone at everything he said.

He reminded me that any expense through tipping would be taken care of when I handed in my expenses at the end of the trip. At the currency exchange booth, I exchanged thirty pounds sterling into roughly nine hundred naira. This seemed to be a lot of money, but there was no way I was going to argue. After I received my cash, my escort took me to the side of the building and whistled and waved to someone in the car park, all the time ensuring that I was never at the edge of the airport front. At the time I wondered why this was. Within a couple of minutes, a car zoomed up. Still holding me back, the driver got out, lifted my case, and put it into the boot. My escort then looked along the edge of the airport front, and within a second, I was whisked into the back passenger seat of the car, the doors were slammed shut, and the car zoomed away. My escort did not get in the car, and I presumed it was only me and the driver until we were outside the airport security system. Outside the airport perimeter, we joined the main dual carriage. Another man appeared in the front passenger seat; he was crouched down and was covered with a dark blanket, and as I was sitting in the back seat, I could not have seen him.

My new unwanted guest after talking to the driver for a brief time turned to me and said, "You are ours now, and you are going to pay big time." At this time, I knew that I was being kidnapped, and I can assure you it was not a good feeling. I felt physically sick at first. I tried to say something, but nothing came out. My mouth went dry as I tried to compose myself. I finally started to speak asked them to take me to the nearest hotel. They said, "That is where we are taking you." They drove up to the hotel, helped me out of the car with my case, and said, "Wait here." Panicking, I approached the desk and asked if I could book a room for the night. There was no chance, as the hotel was fully booked. When I turned round, my two unwanted friends were there with another guy. They lifted my case and escorted me into the same car I had just come out of just outside the main entrance. Why they dropped me off there for that short time I'll never know. While driving away from the hotel, the third gent

Trials and Tribulations of a Travelling Prostitute

said, "Do not worry; you are in good hands now." After a few minutes, I said, "Take me back to the airport and I'll give them money." He replied by saying that it would have to be a lot of money, for his friends expected lots of money. Conversation between me and the kidnappers dried up as we sped along the dual carriageway out of Lagos. After around thirty minutes, the driver veered across the road and went down a dark single-lane road which was very bumpy. Again I tried to convince them to take me to back to the airport. This time there was no feedback.

Being driven quite fast along this narrow one-way street was quite scary, to say the least. Again I tried to start a conversation by asking what speed we were doing, Just at that time, he started to slow down. I was hoping that I was getting through to him, but to my dismay, he said, "We are approaching a village, and if you try to get out, the locals will chop your head off, as there are still head hunters in some villages in Nigeria, and they don't take to kindly to white men." They also informed me that even if I escaped and went to the police, I could be assured that the policemen would take me back to the kidnappers, as they, too, would expect a payment. Not only did the villagers not like white men, but neither did my kidnappers. Driving slowly through the village was more than scary. There were men, women, and children fighting to peer into the car, mostly into the back passenger seat at a frightened white stranger travelling through their village. The horn was blaring all the time so that car could keep moving. Looking through the crowds at the roadside stalls, I realised why I was in this terrible place. The people had no power and no air conditioning, the stalls were illuminated with candles, and they seemed to have absolutely nothing which we living in Scotland took for granted. After finally leaving the village, we travelled for another fifteen minutes again at a speed that was asking for a crash. Eventually the car slowed down and stopped. We were at a clearing in the jungle. At the bottom of the clearing was a large brick wall illuminated by four large floodlights.

They were illuminating not only the wall but also what appeared to be some form of compound. The driver dipped his lights and then flashed his headlamps three times, and the gates facing us opened. Before we drove in, a heavily armed guard brandishing a small machine gun (I was informed later it was called an Uzi) came up to the car and flashed a large beam of light onto the driver and his accomplice and then on me before giving the driver the okay to proceed. When we drove into the compound and the gates shut behind us, I felt as if I were was going to be sick. All my thoughts turned to thinking to myself how on Earth I could possibly escape from here. Even when daylight came, my mind was working overtime. I was thinking of stealing a car and ramming it through the gate; silly things were going through my head, which did not help the situation.

We parked outside one of the building entrances halfway down the compound, and with headlights shining I could clearly see four other men standing about, all carrying the same type of machine gun as that of the guard who had let us into the compound, so all my thoughts of escaping were totally gone. Feeling very much alone and more frightened than before, I sat in the car, wanting to cry. After a brief discussion between the driver and the guards, one of them approached the car and opened the passenger door. Just as he opened the door, all the lighting in the compound went out. Before he could say anything, I said, "Is there a backup generator within the compound?" The answer was no, so I then said, "Please take me to Lagos, any hotel, as they will have power backup." The guard seemed to be taken aback by my request.

He shut the passenger door and walked down the compound, talking to the car's driver. After a lengthy discussion at the bottom of the compound between all the guards, the driver and his associate approached the car once again. Opening the door, the driver said, "Mr. MacKay, you have to go into the building. Your room has been prepared. To his surprise, I said, "No. There is no air conditioning." I explained that I had come from a cold climate and if I went into a room with no air conditioning in this climate, I would probably come down with the flu and would not be able to teach or repair the generator which had obviously failed to produce any power. Again the guard returned to his colleagues, pointing and gesturing in my direction, and yet again I sat in the back of car, wondering what was going to happen next. I was frightened that the next time they came up they would point an automatic gun at me and order me out of the car, and this time I would have to obey, as I could see they were unhappy that I was still staying in the car. Another ten minutes passed with no contact from my kidnappers. Time was dragging by when the compound doors opened behind me and into the compound drove what looked like an old American Cadillac – white with blue accents – in very good condition. It parked behind me, and out stepped a well-dressed gentleman dressed in Nigerian regalia. He walked by my car to the bottom of the compound, where he held an audience with the guards and driver of my car. After his conversation with them, he approached my car, opened the driver's door, sat down, turned around, and said, "Why are you not in your room?" I reiterated exactly what my conversation with the guards had been and asked him to take me to a hotel in Lagos, explaining that I was supposed to travel to the power station at Ughelli tomorrow so that I could get lights on to the compound and villages here in Nigeria. He got up from the front seat, slammed the door of the car, and walked down the compound, flashing his bull whip vigorously as he walked. He stopped at the bottom wall, where a deep discussion took place. This conversation seemed to be quite heated, and one of the guards produced a pistol, which made me very frightened. He seemed to cock it a couple of times and then put it away.

Just when I was feeling a little tired, my kidnapper came up to the car, walked by me, opened the boot, removed my case, and placed it in the boot of the Mustang. After closing it, he hurriedly ran down the compound. As soon as he was at the bottom, I left the back seat of my car and jumped into the back seat of the Mustang. In my eyes, if any car was to leave the compound, it had to be this one, and I wanted to leave with it. My well-dressed Nigerian gentleman came up and sat in the car, and we had a discussion. I explained my position and said that he had to look after me, as it was his company which generated the request that I should visit Nigeria and teach the local engineers to operate and maintain the gas turbine so that lights could be switched on. If they tripped again, I told him that they could then repair the machines themselves without asking for outside assistance. Explaining to him who I was and what I was doing in Nigeria seemed to set him back a little, as if he had been expecting someone else. I still maintained the pretence that it was his company that had sent for me to come and work here, meaning that I was his responsibility and he had to look after me. He left the car and called over his guards. They had a discussion. After the conversation, some of them jumped into the car I had come in. One single guard went into the back passenger seat of the car I was in through the driver's door, and the other guards opened up the compound gate. After about five minutes, my Nigerian host jumped into the driver's seat and we reversed out. My only reservation was that the guard sitting in the passenger seat was the one with the revolver, which he later produced and held to my head. He told me to keep quiet, obviously adhering to his orders to speak only when asked to do so. Driving along the road in which I arrived, my driver realised just how bumpy the road was and drove with a lot more care and attention than my original driver. This, for some reason, seemed to give me a little bit of comfort – in fact a whole lot of comfort. It was not to the degree that I felt totally safe; I just knew my driver was worried about his life and was not going to do anything that would cause him any harm, and that meant I was reasonably safe with him. As we were coming through the bush, my eyes lit up when we approached the main motorway and I saw that the street lights were illuminated.

The relief of being away from the jungle and in some sort of normality was heaven. We turned onto the main motorway and headed south back to Lagos, only to turn off the motorway again after four hundred yards. We turned right into a motel, where we parked at the very back. There was the main building. I could see six outbuildings on the opposite side, and I presumed there were six on the other side and two at the bottom, arranged like a cul-de-sac. All the guards from the other car and my host went into the reception area; that left my handgun-toting friend and me sitting and not speaking for more than ten minutes. He clicked the revolver every couple of minutes. The wait was excruciating. From the reception area, two of the guards came out and turned left and then left again down the cul-de-sac. Five minutes later, all the remaining men appeared, jumped into the cars, and slowly drove, following in the footsteps of the two guards. They stopped at the bottom, and everyone was ushered into the one of the outbuildings. This included me. The door was shut behind us. I thought the hinges were going to come off, but then everyone seemed to be a little bit more relaxed, including myself. With everyone looking for a place to sit, I ended up facing my Nigerian host. Then, suddenly, the door opened and one of my captives carried in my cases and left them on the floor. I immediately jumped up, opened my case, and presented the hosts with a folder containing all the correspondence between my company and his main office (still pretending that he belonged to the company which had brought me to Nigeria). He read through the latest emails and said, "This is all very good, but you do not travel all the way to Nigeria with no money." I showed what was left of the two hundred pounds that I originally came with. It was snatched from my hand by one of the guards, and that was the last I saw of that. I sat back down, hoping that everything I explained as to why I was there and my reason for not having a lot of money was accepted and they would leave me alone so that I would have time to think. I was rudely awakened when my gun-toting friend pressed the gun against my temple and shouted, "Bang!" This was a setback. I then said, feeling that frustration was growing among my hosts because the money they had taken was not enough, that I could get more money, trying to calm the situation. "I will have to go to the office tomorrow in Lagos," I said, "and they can send a message to Scotland to send it.

This I can't do till the morning, and bearing in mind tomorrow is Saturday, I can only hope that they will be open. As I have said, all my correspondence has been through your company." This comment prompted a debate among all the Nigerians in the room, though it was in a local language I was not privy to. Suddenly my host rose and insisted that all others should leave the room. As he left, he turned to me and said, "Tomorrow we will go to Lagos." As he left, though I was physically drained, I somehow shoved the cabinet against the door and shoved the bed against the cabinet. I was determined that they were not going to get into the room ever again. I fell back on the bed, and the phone rang. At the other end was my host, telling me that if I required breakfast or anything else, I was to phone 17, which was reception, and my requirements would be taken care of. Based on that phone call, I presumed that they were close by and probably watching my room, as 17 is never generally a reception number. Reception usually uses a single number, which makes it easier for guest to remember. As I returned to my position on the bed, my head was in a spin. Not knowing what to do was the hardest thing to grasp. All the paperwork I had shown to my hosts to explain why I was in Nigeria they had taken away. All the money I had they had stolen from me. The only way to get more money was my American Express credit card, and I was banking on that saving me tomorrow. Getting up from the bed to a sitting position, I started to plot my escape, checking round the room to see if there was an address which told me where I was. Nothing was evident. I looked through the drawers and found a rolled-up laundry slip. This I put in a safe place beside my credit card so I could give it to a bank clerk or someone to let them know where I had been, if it could be used to trace my movements. After my search, I sat back down on the bed, thinking, what should I do? At two o'clock in the morning, after travelling all day, my mind was still racing. Two things came to mind. Firstly, if they were watching me from another room, then I needed to keep my lights on as long as possible and hope that when I switched them off they would presume that I was going to sleep, prompting them to do the same.

Secondly, there was no chance of leaving this room until it starts to get light, going by what I was told about head hunters. With these two points in the back of my mind, I searched around all the windows, which had bars and shutters on them, ensuring no one could break in – or, in my case, that no one could break out. I checked the toilet shutter and found a quite significant crack at the bottom; this would let me see when it became light. After waiting till 3.30 am, I switched of all the lights in my room. I hoped this would send a signal to my captors that I was trying to get some sleep and they would do the same. There was no way that I could sleep while believing people that could do me harm were only a couple of doors away, so for the rest of night, I sat and watched the toilet window, waiting for dawn. My plan was to remove all the furniture from the door when dawn came, creep out, jump into the massive drain running down the side of the buildings, crawl up to the reception area, and demand them to order a taxi to take me to the British Embassy. Sitting for three hours looking at a window and worrying what could happen was not my idea of an enjoyable new-country experience. The minutes ticked by very slowly, and eventually there was light.

I quickly removed all the obstacles put against the door and opened the door slowly, holding on to my case. In the event that guards were outside my door, I was going to throw the case at them and then run to the reception area, Thankfully no one was outside my door, exactly as I had planned, I jumped into the drain, crouched down, and made my way to the top of the lane, where I waited for a couple of minutes to get my breath back and calm down. After leaving the drain, I ran across the driveway to reception, where I ran into a local boy. I shouting at him, saying I had been kidnapped and was being kept against my will and needed a taxi to take me to the British Embassy. The local boy ran from the motel, and within minutes he came back with a taxi – an old Morris

Minor. My heart was racing. I opened the passenger door and jumped in, shouting, "British Embassy – now!" The taxi swung out of the motel and joined the main motorway. Just as I was feeling a little bit safer, the taxi stopped. "Puncture," the driver said. I was in a panic, thinking this was a setup. I jumped from the taxi, ready to run down the motorway. When I looked down at the back wheel, I saw that he indeed did have a puncture. I opened the boot, removed the spare, and changed the wheel in minutes.

Motor racing crews would have been proud of my expertise and quickness in changing the wheel, wheel changed, we set off again into Lagos, and within a short period of time we were outside the British Embassy. You have no idea how relieved I was. Seeing the Union Jack flying proudly outside made me feel safe for the first time in twelve hours.

I went up to the entrance, where a guard contacted one of the embassy personnel. He came out explaining the situation. He knew all about me, saying, "We got a report last night that you had been abducted from the airport and were awaiting a ransom demand this morning." I explained that the taxi driver that took me here had not been paid and asked if someone could go out and pay him or if I could borrow some money to pay him. He informed me that it would be taken care of. After a couple of hours and a few cups of coffee, embassy staff took me to a down town hotel, booked me in, and said that my client would come to my room in the afternoon. This would give me a little time to unwind and have a couple of hours sleep after my experience.

Looking out from my window, I could see armoured personnel carriers on two sides of the hotel, along with plenty of soldiers with automatic weapons. This put me at ease. I showered, lay down on the bed, and slept for a couple of hours. Around two o'clock, my phone rang. The client introduced himself and asked me down for lunch. I agreed, with the sole intention of telling them that I was leaving Nigeria and would not be back. On entering the foyer, three gents approached and introduced themselves. They were very apologetic regarding the mix-up at the airport and assured me that they had been outside but had not envisioned me being taken out through the diplomatic exit. Accepting the grovelling apology, I said that I wanted to leave and asked that they please arrange for the flight as soon as possible. They asked me to reconsider, as it would take a couple of days to arrange a departure visa. Also, I was unharmed and was now in safe hands. They took great care in explaining that the abductees would not try to abduct me again, as I had proven to them it would not be worth their while, as I had no money of significant value that would interest them. "That's what they wanted – money. They did not want to harm you, as it would have been easy to do. All they wanted was money." The client went on explaining that Nigeria desperately needed people like me to fix things and teach and train local Nigerians on how to keep the lights on. The power stations were continually being closed down because of lack of expertise, and my visit to Ughelli would be greatly appreciated. They said that I would be taken to a protected camp by a convoy of four by-fours and be protected twenty-four hours a day. After listening to this and remembering my experience in the bush, during which I saw many villages that had no electricity (and those that did were continually faced with power cuts), I decided to go and complete my assignment. It was arranged that we would leave the following morning at nine o'clock. They would phone at eight, and we would have breakfast before leaving. This would give me a whole night to rest and think about whether I was doing the right thing.

The rest of the day and night passed very slowly. The hotel was very basic. It definitely needed a lot of work, but the overall assessment was that it was clean and safe, and it was only for one night, as I had been in worse places. It was not a chore spending the night there. Morning came. I was up, showered, and awaiting the eight o'clock phone call, and it was on time. I made my way down to the breakfast area, apprehensive about what the next weeks were going to produce. I was met at the lift area by the client, and my case was taken from me and put in a four-by-four at the hotel's front door. I was then escorted to the dining room and had breakfast. We set off around nine. Everything appeared well, and I had settled down, knowing that the three four-by-fours in the convoy meant everything I had been promised was being carried out. This seemed to be too good to be true. At the protected camp, the security guard let us through the barrier. We stopped at the front of the main building, and the client went in to register our arrival. On his exit from the building, he handed me key number one and pointed to the chalet nearby, carrying my case to the door. He informed me that they would be staying in chalets five, six, and eight. We would meet up again in a couple of hours for something to eat.

The chalet was clean. It had a fridge, kettle, and tea- and coffee making facilities. I lay back on the bed, thinking that I was glad that I had decided to fulfil the company's commitment. Leaving the chalet, I was confronted with a frightening experience a security guard patrolling the grounds with a bow and arrow. Walking briskly to the restaurant, sat down, and told the client about my experience. He explained that he had just been informed that there had been a riot in Benin, not far from here, and that troops had removed all guns from the security people. I expressed my concern that I had just left abductors which had weapons that easily matched bows and arrows and that if they were looking for me, I did not think the battle would last long. My client assured me that what happened at the airport was over. The people who took me wanted money, he told me, and when they realised that I could not give them the money they needed, they let me go. He also explained to me that his company did not have a bank account in Nigeria but generally brought in money via various office staff, and it so happened that my name matched that of one of their employees. "The kidnappers probably have all our employees' names and matched your name with one of them and presumed that you were carrying money lots of money.

When they realised that their assumption was way off the mark, they knew they would have to live with disappointment until the next time, as you were not the first nor will be the last to be abducted." A British minister had already suffered the same fate. He had been released as well, after giving up his wallet and watch. The next morning, travelling to the site was quite easy, as it was just across the road, which was good for me. After taking me to the power station, my escort said that they were travelling back to Lagos and that I would be picked up at 1700 hours and taken back to the compound. As they left, I felt a little exposed. This feeling evaporated when I met the site superintendent. We had a lengthy chat. This experience was very assuring. He expressed his deep thanks for coming to his power station after all I had been through. He said that if it had been him, he would have been on the first flight home as soon as he could get one. He then took me to a reception room where I met ten employees who were going to be my students for the next two weeks. They were all established engineers in their own right, and we got on very well. On opening the lessons, each engineer had a few questions relating to the problems on site. These were compiled, and I informed them that each of their concerns and questions would be covered and answered before I left the site. That evening when I went for dinner, there were two other British engineers, and I was introduced to them both. They were residents in Nigeria working for a glass company. Both appeared to be genuine guys, so we had a chat, and everything was going well until the drink kicked in. When you are working abroad and you are dealing with people who are paying a lot of money to have you there, the last thing they want is you turning up for work stinking of stale booze, so one of my strict rules was to have a pint or two but no more. When I informed my two new friends that this was my policy, their attitude seemed to change. I informed them that this was my policy and that it did not bother me how much other people consumed, as in Glasgow we had always different levels of alcohol intake among a squad of pals. With the attitude between my new friends not being the best, I made a point of not being in their company every night, making excuses like checking up on problems at the site. And by the way, this was not very far from the truth, as the machines were not in the best of shape, between sand in the inlet and dirt in the control cab and panel. My job was not straightforward. Nigerian people are generally very welcoming, but there is still a big problem in the country with the wealth not being distributed evenly among all citizens. There are a lot of very, very poor people – something we do not have in Britain. What I mean by "very, very poor people" is children who do not have any shoes and wash in the street in dirty water. I witnessed all this one weekend when I was informed that the power station was closing down for vital repairs on Sunday and that the engineers being taught by me were required for other duties, meaning I was not required. As I was not working Sunday, I was invited to come with my new friends to Benin, were there was a market and I could buy some odds and ends. I thought initially that this was a bad idea, but I went along. As we drove along, the poverty was very evident. When I saw very dirty children risking their lives for scraps, it did pull at my heartstrings. If that was bad, what was waiting for me round the next bend was even more harrowing. There was a body lying at the side of the road with no head. The body was wearing a light fawn overall, which was dark down to his knees because of the blood.

Trials and Tribulations of a Travelling Prostitute

The only bit that was fawn was a bit between his knees and the tops of his rigger boots. I turned away before I saw his neck. My new friends informed me that there were some tribes still performing amputations of the head, classing themselves as head-hunters. This unfortunate man had been just walking along the road when attacked. His head had been severed, and his body had been returned and dumped at the side of the road. It was horrific, and I may say I felt sick at thought of it. It also brought my thinking back to when I was abducted from the airport. My captive did say that if I tried to jump out of the car, I would most certainly be killed by the locals. On arriving in Benin's market area, we all purchased some items and, to be quite honest, had a good laugh. This shows that when too much drink is consumed, people don't really enjoy themselves as much as they do when sober. After purchasing our goods (my friends purchased a lot more than I), as their drinking habits had been honed for many years, we went to a bar. To my surprise, it was full of ex-pats: Germans, Dutch, and British. And we had a ball. Driving back to Ughelli, we passed the unfortunate guy who had run into the head-hunters, only this time he was naked and was wearing no boots. Someone had stripped him of his only possessions and just left him there. This was poverty. When I returned to work Monday, my students explained about the head-hunters. They didn't do it every day, but only on very rare occasions. I found that very assuring. On completing my duties, three machines were delivering full power and two were producing 60 per cent power. This was a complete success, considering that only two machines were producing 50 per cent power when I arrived. I again thought back to my abduction, when all the compounds and villages around were put in complete darkness every night. I felt a great sense of satisfaction that the power needed had been restored by my efforts. Having received an email explaining that a driver was on his way to pick me up and take me to the Lagos airport, I felt wonderful saying my farewells to the employees of the power station. By the way, they were excellent in their application and their respect for me, and I could not thank them enough. I walked across the road to the compound, packed, and awaited my car. When it arrived, it was late afternoon. It was decided that he would stay the night and drive in the morning. That would not be a problem, as my flight was not till the afternoon anyway. When morning came, I was bright-eyed and bushy-tailed, knowing that I was heading home. I thought to myself, what could happen now? Nothing I thought. We set out early with no problems. Driving along the same road, we came to what I would call a large piece of wasteland which was meant to be a roundabout, but no one there had any idea as to how a roundabout worked. It was a free-for-all, with people shooting across. It was scary. My driver, trying to be very careful – probably because I was there – sat for a good five minutes, waiting for a clearing before entering the roundabout. As we were taking the third exit, we finally made it onto the roundabout. Just before leaving, a policeman appeared with his hand up, signaling my driver to stop.

The driver stood on the brake pedal, and I said to him, "Do not stop here; we will be killed. Pull over to the side of the road just to the left of the policeman." This he did, and we stopped. The policeman pulled out his gun and pointed it at my head. "Why did you not stop?" he said. The driver was shaking, and I said, "We have stopped. We could not stop immediately; as you can see, there are a lot of cars on the roundabout." After a three- or four-minute discussion, he said, "I'm taking you to my police station." I said, "Why? We have not done anything wrong." He replied by saying, "You will not like my police station." He then jumped into the back seat of the car, his revolver at the back of my head. Again he said, "You will not like my police station." Again I repeated myself by saying that we had done nothing wrong, calculating the predicament I was in. Going to a police station when I had a plane to catch was not a good idea. Bearing in mind that during my short stay in Nigeria, everyone I had met was corrupt, I assumed this policeman was looking for a bribe. After we had travelled a short distance, I turned round and said, "Why can't we be friends?" He replied by saying we should be friends. Biting the bullet, I said, "How much will this friendship cost?" he replied, "Fifty naira." I scrambled about in my pocket, not wanting to let him know how much money I had. I produced two twenty-naira notes and said, "Would forty naira be enough for friendship?" He took the money, told the driver to stop, and jumped out, and we drove away. I was left thinking that I had just had a cocked revolver pointed at my head for the second time on this trip and could have easily have been killed for around £1.40. This summed up the poverty and desperation in the country. After being delayed by the policeman while travelling back to Lagos, I informed the driver to take

Trials and Tribulations of a Travelling Prostitute

me directly to the airport. I was adamant that under no circumstances was I was returning to Lagos informing the driver that I would forward my report to the chief engineer when I arrived back in the United Kingdom. The airport experience was something to behold. After checking in, there were five security screenings before I got to the departure lounge. At each station, I had to hand over some form of payment. As the money was useless anyway, it was not a problem to get rid of some notes. The only problem was that as there were five stations, I had given away all my Nigerian cash by the time I arrived at the departure gate. "Not a problem," I said. "The next step will be to sit back on the plane with a nice, cold beer."

The plane arrived and parked about one hundred yards from the departure lounge. All passengers were informed to go down to the runway and identify their luggage and then return to the departure lounge. So, like all good passengers, we obeyed. A young Nigerian came over and said, "Your case?" I said yes, and as usual, the hand was out. I explained to him that I did not have any cash left, as I had given it all away getting to the departure lounge. This information was greeted with "Well, you'll pay." When in London, I got my case back, and it looked as if it must have been kicked all one hundred yards to the aeroplane. When the plane touched down in London, I said a little prayer in relief at being back in the United Kingdom, where law and order are taken for granted by most people. Only after you experience corruption and lawlessness in the likes of Nigeria can you appreciate that what we have in the United Kingdom should never be compromised. On arriving back at the company, I logged my report, demanding answers as to why I had been allowed to travel to a country which had major problems with crime. I then found out more about the management deputation that went to Nigeria, travelled to the site, and returned with feedback that there was nothing to report. What they failed to disclose in their report was that they had never reached the site. Halfway to the site, there was a rowdy demonstration which became quite violent, and some people were badly injured. The delegation turned back to Lagos and conjured up a plan to work while sitting in a hotel room. This plan was a total fabrication, as the information that they were given was more than a month old, and the machines on site were not in good working order and required major work. Again a meeting was called by my manager, and invited to attend was the management team that had taken the order and travelled to Nigeria. As might have guessed, only the personnel manager appeared, offering the company's sincere regret for what happened. You can imagine how I felt. I went out wanting to do my best, and after having put up with a terrible situation, no one came forward and apologised. At least he said they would put things in place so it would never happen again. Five days later, a phone call came from the personnel department. I was to go up and have a chat with the personnel director. After the discussion, he said that the company had decided to give me an extra day of holiday. Well, what could I say. My life was put at risk because management refused to travel to the site, and they gave me an extra day of holiday. This was also a fabrication. The real reason for my extra day of holiday was the letter they received from BEI, which read as follows:

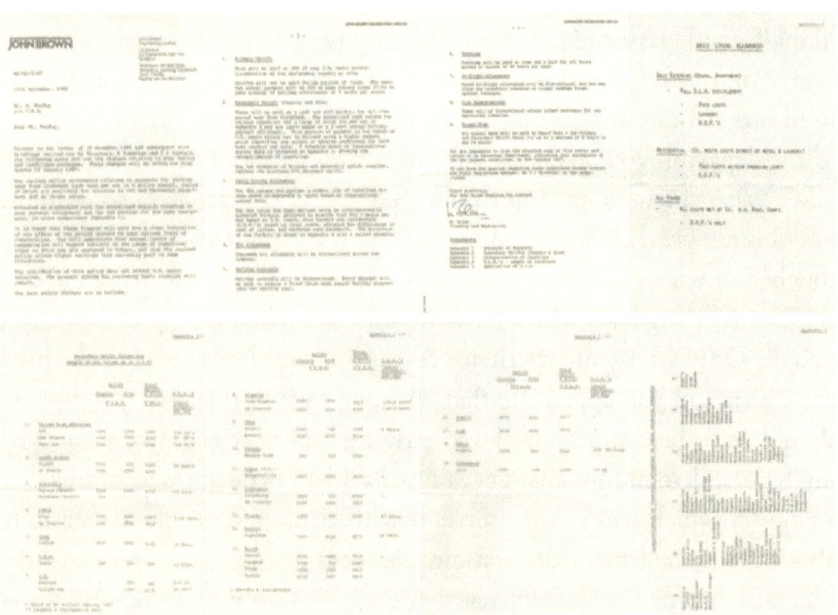

New Contract Details

Trials and Tribulations of a Travelling Prostitute

```
              INTRODUCTION OF REVISED OVERSEAS & OFF-SITE CONDITIONS

    NAME/NO.  A. MACKAY  (2047)         JOB TITLE   RESIDENT ENGINEER

    BASE SALARY   11008.53              JOB GRADE   07D

    COUNTRY       AUSTRALIA

    SITE          CHANNEL ISLANDS


    PRESENT PACKAGE                     NEW PACKAGE (FROM 19/01/87)

                    £                                                £

    BASE SALARY   =   11008.53          BASE SALARY          =   11008.53
    55% OF BASE                         (A) PRIMARY
    x 44/52       =    5123.20              (20% of BASE) = 2201.71

                                        (B) SECONDARY     = 1000
                                                          = 2000

                                        (A + B) x 47/52   =    4701.55

                      £16131.73                               £15710.08


    DLA @ 44 WEEKS                      DLA AT 47 WEEKS
    (N45 x 44 x 7) =   6468             (N23 x 47 x 7) =        3619
    £21                                 £11


    TOTAL         =   £22599.73         TOTAL          =       £19329.08


    PREPARED BY :  _____      DATE :  _____
```

Contract New Pricing

I left his office not knowing what to think. At first I felt disbelief, and then I thought, Is that all I'm worth to an international company who sends people all over the world, practically on a daily basis, charging well over the rate per day for my services? I stopped and thought, If worse came to worst and I had been killed, would they have paid my wife for the extra holiday I couldn't have taken? During my time home, I had a good chat with a fellow colleague who had gone to Nigeria before I did. As management had said to me, he had had no problems apart from the secure accommodation and food – the latter of which was very basic and not the best; we both were in agreement about that. He was surprised that I had

had so much hassle. They still did not grasp that the people who abducted me from the airport knew BEI was bringing in another engineer whose name was on the airline passenger list (my name) and were expecting me to be carrying money – a lot of money. BEI knew abduction was common in Nigeria, so why did they not have someone inside the baggage area looking out for me? Even after the event and after they sent the letter, they were still in denial about what actually happened. They made a mess of it, and as they did not want any backlash, they came up with the letter, which was pathetic. My having been held at gunpoint and interrogated in a hotel

www.ingramcontent.com/pod-product-compliance
Lightning Source LLC
Chambersburg PA
CBHW030853180526
45163CB00004B/1552